T0105166

The Book of
Reading
and
Writing

Ideas, Tips, and Lists
for the
Elementary
Classroom

*To my family and friends for their love,
encouragement, and support.*

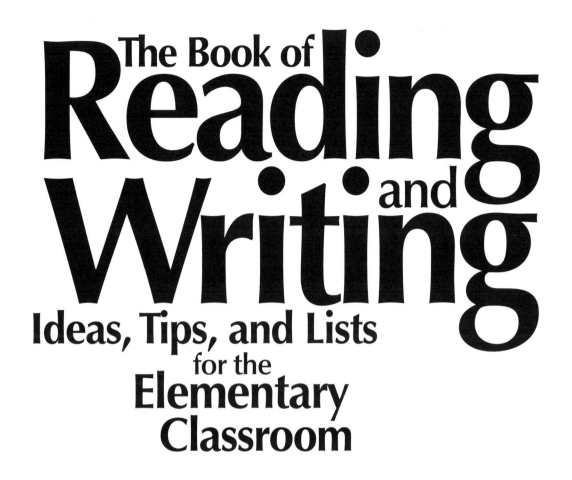

The Book of
Reading and Writing

Ideas, Tips, and Lists
for the
Elementary
Classroom

SANDRA ANDERSON

Skyhorse Publishing

Copyright © 2003 by Sandra Anderson

First Skyhorse Publishing edition 2014

All rights reserved. No part of this book may be reproduced in any manner without the express written consent of the publisher, except in the case of brief excerpts in critical reviews or articles. All inquiries should be addressed to Skyhorse Publishing, 307 West 36th Street, 11th Floor, New York, NY 10018.

Skyhorse Publishing books may be purchased in bulk at special discounts for sales promotion, corporate gifts, fund-raising, or educational purposes. Special editions can also be created to specifications. For details, contact the Special Sales Department, Skyhorse Publishing, 307 West 36th Street, 11th Floor, New York, NY 10018 or info@skyhorsepublishing.com.

Skyhorse® and Skyhorse Publishing® are registered trademarks of Skyhorse Publishing, Inc.®, a Delaware corporation.

Visit our website at www.skyhorsepublishing.com.

10 9 8 7 6 5 4 3 2 1

Library of Congress Cataloging-in-Publication Data is available on file.

Cover design by Tracy E. Miller

ISBN: 978-1-62914-670-6
Ebook ISBN: 978-1-62914-879-3

Printed in China

Contents

About the Author

 **Sandra E. Anderson** is an educational consultant with Exemplary Education L.L.C., which offers training in strengthening reading and writing achievement and enhancing leadership for literacy. As a former teacher, reading specialist, principal, and national staff development director, she is passionate about literacy education. She is an experienced presenter at state, regional, and national reading and writing conferences. In addition, she has been a consultant for several reading textbook companies. The Washington State Elementary Principals Association honored Anderson as an outstanding instructional leader. She was a member of the International Reading Association's Teachers' Choices Committee for four years. She received her B.A. in Education from the University of Washington and M.A. degrees in Reading and Educational Administration from Seattle Pacific University. Throughout her career her focus has been on practical ideas that can make a difference for teachers and students.

Introduction

For students to receive the best possible education, all educators must focus on improving literacy instruction across the grades. Even with what we know about effective instructional practices, a significant number of students are not reading and writing on grade level. This book approaches reading and writing programs as if looking through two camera lenses. The first is a wide-angle view looking at the big picture, including effective schools research and the critical components of a complete, comprehensive reading and writing program. The second lens is a zoom lens focusing in on specific ideas, tips, and suggestions for strengthening students' reading and writing performance. Each chapter provides practical ideas and resources designed for new and experienced elementary teachers, reading specialists, administrators, staff developers, and directors of curriculum and instruction. This resource book may be especially valuable for beginning teachers or those working with beginning teachers.

Chapter 1 identifies the **key characteristics of effective schools** and discusses practical ways of using what we know about effective schools and effective teachers to positively impact reading and writing programs.

Chapter 2 looks at the **components necessary for an effective, complete reading program**. It provides specific ideas and tips for reading aloud, shared reading, guided reading, literacy centers, literature circles, and independent reading.

Chapter 3 focuses on the **essential elements of reading instruction**. Numerous strategies and innovations are presented for teaching phonemic awareness, phonics, high-frequency sight words, vocabulary, language structure, fluency, and comprehension.

Chapter 4 includes the five components necessary for an **effective, complete writing program**. There are ideas and innovations for modeled writing, interactive writing, structured writing, writers workshops, and independent writing.

Chapter 5 discusses **how writing skills should be taught** in context, either using reading as a model or using students' writing as examples. Numerous ideas are presented for teaching writing content, use of language, mechanics, and revision and editing.

Chapter 6 looks at other **instructional factors impacting the success of a reading and writing program** including the use of instructional time, the selection of instructional materials, the use of a print-rich environment for instruction, and the incorporation of a wide variety of assessments.

Chapter 7 provides specific suggestions for **safety nets that make a difference for struggling readers**. It provides multiple options that any school or teacher can use to strengthen the reading and writing performance of struggling readers.

Chapter 8 includes **recommendations for information gathering and data collection**. By collecting and utilizing pertinent data, teachers can focus instruction on the areas that will have the greatest impact on students' reading and writing performance.

Chapter 9 provides **practical ideas for staff training in literacy practices**. These are time-efficient, easy-to-use training tips that can be easily adapted to different school settings.

Chapter 10 describes **fifty 10-minute tips** that any school leaders, including principals, reading specialists, or teacher leaders, can use to impact the reading and writing performance of students.

Chapter 11 provides **101 ideas for involving parents and families** in a school's literacy program.

Successful, high-performing schools have incorporated the research on effective schools and successful literacy practices. Educators working together can have even greater impact. The goal of this book is to provide practical, research-based ideas that will help teachers strengthen their students' reading and writing performance.

Chapter 1
A Practical Look at Literacy and Effective School Practices

> **Success Story**
>
> *A large, low-performing elementary school focused on effective school practices and literacy for 3 years. This included extensive staff development, teacher observations during literacy instruction, and purchasing literacy materials. At the end of the third year, students demonstrated significant gains in reading and writing when assessed on several different measures. Book sets that had been read by fifth graders were given to the third-grade classrooms.*

Effective school practices are critical to enhancing students' reading and writing performance. Implementing effective literacy practices without addressing effective school practices will not provide maximum results. The key characteristics of schools that have successful literacy programs include the following.

EFFECTIVE PRACTICE 1

STUDENT-CENTERED SCHOOLS
The school is student centered and has high expectations for all students.

Schools that are achieving outstanding results in reading and writing are focused on the literacy needs of students.

A. Students have a strong sense of belonging.

- All students are known by name.
- Adults have strong, positive relationships with students.
- There is a positive, safe, and orderly environment with mutual respect, trust, and equity.
- There is a procedure for welcoming new students.

TIP 1: **Photographs** of new students can be placed on a photo wall in a staff area with the student's name, teacher, and an interest. This is an easy way for all staff members to get to know new students and also ensures that new students feel welcome.

TIP 2: New students can be given a **coupon book**. Each coupon is taken to different staff members, such as the librarian, secretary, and special teachers, and traded for a welcoming item. This provides an opportunity for new students to meet staff members.

B. **All students are expected to reach their individual potential.**

C. **The school focuses on students' cognitive and affective needs.**

EXAMPLE: One school found it was insightful to ask parents to identify the student's academic strengths and areas of concern. Teachers found the parent surveys to be incredibly valuable.

EFFECTIVE PRACTICE 2

SHARED PURPOSE AND VISION
There is a shared purpose and vision.

There are clear goals and high expectations focusing on improving students' reading and writing.

A. **The school's goals are obvious to everyone.** The focus is on improving as well as inspiring students' reading and writing through research-based, quality instruction. There is a passion for literacy that is reflected in the school's goals.

TIP1: Goals can be enlarged to poster size and posted around school.

TIP 2: Literacy goals can be printed on business cards and handed out to parents and community members.

B. **Staff development focuses on literacy development.**

TIP: Staff development can be provided in many different formats including staff meetings, book study groups, workshops, and brown bag lunch discussions.

C. **There is a focus on reading and writing.**

TIP 1: Students can be highly involved in literacy activities including writing book reviews that are published in newsletters, videotaping book commercials, and making recommendations for book purchases.

TIP 2: Recommended at-home reading lists can be developed for each instructional level and sent to families. Numerous examples of leveled book lists can be found at www.argotlibrary.com.

D. Students' reading and writing are showcased.

> TIP: Student work can be displayed with goal or objective identified. Another option is to display the student work with the objective covered so parents can guess which goal is being worked on. Parents could then self-check to see if they correctly identified the literacy goal. This keeps students, staff, and parents focused on the school's literacy goals.

E. Every child's progress in reading and writing is seen as everyone's responsibility.

> TIP: Documentation can be kept on each child showing progress or growth over time. One possibility is having students tape record their reading three times during each school year. Students and parents can hear the improvement.

EFFECTIVE PRACTICE 3

STRONG INSTRUCTIONAL LEADERSHIP
There is strong instructional leadership with frequent monitoring of teaching and learning.

Exemplary instructional leaders are master teachers with expert knowledge of teaching strategies, curriculum content, classroom management, and child development. The principal is one of the instructional leaders, but others may also serve as instructional leaders.

A. The principal can have great impact. He or she can link teacher observations and evaluations to the school's instructional goals.

> TIP: Frequent formal and informal classroom observations can be followed up with short discussions, coaching sessions, or notes.

> EXAMPLE: Walk-throughs or brief classroom visits occurred weekly during literacy instruction and were followed with the question, "How does what you're doing help achieve our literacy goals?" This kept the leader aware of what was happening in the classroom and kept teachers and students focused on literacy goals.

B. The instructional leader creates a climate of high expectations, trust, and open communication where collaboration is present and valued. Teachers are encouraged to express their ideas and take risks.

> TIP: To free up staff development time at staff meetings, weekly feedback bulletins can be sent to staff asking for their input. This minimizes the amount of discussion time needed at staff meetings.

> EXAMPLE: As necessary, staff members were given a sheet of response items on Friday and asked to return the sheet by Tuesday morning. This information was summarized prior to Wednesday staff meetings. If a discussion was needed, it could be dealt with quickly. Often the input resulted in a decision where little or no discussion was needed. The time saved was used for staff development.

C. The instructional leader continually monitors students' progress on instructional goals.

> TIP: The instructional leader can collect and present data that will guide literacy instructional practices. The staff can decide which areas should be addressed or what changes should occur based on the data.

> TIP: The instructional leader can keep the focus on literacy achievement by consistently asking, "Will this improve literacy achievement?"

D. Effective instructional practices are modeled.

> TIP: New instructional strategies can be modeled and used during staff meetings as a part of staff development.

> EXAMPLE: A Literacy Focus Group was established where grade-level teams shared a strategy that had been particularly effective for them. This same idea can be used by a district where each school shares literacy successes. These ideas can be put into newsletters or a booklet to be shared with parents and the community.

E. The instructional leader is visible to staff, students, and parents.

EFFECTIVE PRACTICE 4

KNOWLEDGEABLE STAFF MEMBERS
There are knowledgeable staff members who use effective classroom practices.

A. Staff members have strong, positive relationships with students and expect all students to achieve.

- There is a **sense of community** and a feeling that all students belong.
- Students are **highly engaged** in learning and are encouraged to become responsible for their own learning.

  > TIP: Students write their own short-term goals and then assess their success in meeting these goals.

- There are **high expectations** for students, and when students have difficulty there is a redoubling of teaching efforts and/or a seeking of new ways of impacting the learning. Teachers know the strengths and weaknesses of each individual student and take these into consideration when planning instruction.

  > TIP: Differentiated instruction can be used to provide initial teaching and re-teaching. By changing the pace, varying the level, or use a variety of instructional strategies, students can experience greater success.

- Teachers **enjoy** teaching.

B. Staff members use effective and reflective instructional practices.

- Teachers plan activities that will **build on students' prior knowledge**.

  TIP: If the students do not have prior knowledge, the teacher can plan activities to develop the necessary background knowledge so students will experience greater success.

- Students' **interests are considered**—even when teaching required curriculum.

- Students understand **what they are learning and why** they are learning it.

- There is **explicit modeling** and scaffolding.

- There is **frequent monitoring** of students' understanding, and students receive regular, specific, and appropriate feedback.

- A wide **variety of instructional strategies**, methods, and materials are utilized.

- Teachers **use the latest research** on differentiated instruction, multiple intelligences, and brain research in providing the best possible instruction.

- Teachers **vary their teaching styles** from direct instruction to coaching.

- **Higher-level thinking** is a consistent part of the instruction.

- Teachers **reflect** on their lessons and make changes to strengthen learning.

C. Staff members have knowledge of effective literacy practices.

- A **balanced**, complete reading and writing program is taught.

- Students' literacy **needs are identified** and lessons are planned to meet these needs.

- **Assessment** of students' progress is done on an ongoing basis, and this information is used in planning literacy instruction.

- Teachers **reflect** on the successes and challenges of literacy lessons.

- Teachers have **knowledge of materials**, including children's literature.

D. Staff members use effective classroom management skills.

  TIP: Research (Taylor, Pearson, Clark, and Walpole, 2000) has found that those classrooms that have the most effective reading programs have 95% on-task behaviors.

- Students are **involved in developing the rules** and procedures for the classroom. Students review and practice classroom rules and procedures as often as necessary.

  TIP: Classroom management is most effective when the following questions have been addressed. Do the students know what they should be doing during the literacy blocks? Do they know how to get their questions answered? Do they know what to do when they are not to interrupt the teacher, such as during guided reading groups?

- Teachers are **consistent in enforcing the rules** and procedures. Visual cues may be used when teachers are not to be interrupted, such as during guided reading.

  EXAMPLE: One teacher wore special glasses when she was not to be interrupted. The students used other options during this time, such as asking another student. The visual cue was effective in reducing interruptions.

- **Transitions are smooth** and time effective. Goals are set to minimize the amount of time spent in transition.

    EXAMPLES: One classroom charted the amount of time it took for transitions. Students attempted to "beat their previous time" and reduced their transition times to less than one minute. Another teacher played part of a song and students completed the transition by the time the music stopped.

EFFECTIVE PRACTICE 5

ALIGNMENT OF CURRICULUM, INSTRUCTION, AND ASSESSMENT
Curriculum, instruction, and assessment are in alignment.

Schools achieving the greatest success in improving reading and writing performance have evaluated their literacy programs to ensure that instruction, curriculum, and assessment are in alignment.

A. **Schools evaluate their success in meeting the standards at each grade level.**

    EXAMPLE: Each grade level identified areas where student performance was of concern. They then looked for patterns across the grades. This led to discussions and decisions about changes that should be made in instruction and materials.

B. **Instruction should be designed to meet students' needs as well as teach the curriculum.**

    EXAMPLE: Teachers used differentiated instructional strategies and created multiple options for the same curriculum content. This led to greater student success, yet ensured that all students were learning the content.

C. **Assessment should always take into consideration two factors—does it match the content that is being taught and does it assess the learning in the same way the instruction has been presented?**

    EXAMPLE: Students were scoring low on the spelling section of a standardized test. When the test was evaluated, the staff realized that the test assessed proofreading skills and little of their spelling instruction had focused on proofreading. When instruction was changed to include more proofreading, the scores went up dramatically.

EFFECTIVE PRACTICE 6

INFORMATION AND DATA COLLECTION
A wide variety of information and data are collected and utilized when making instructional decisions.

Data can be used to show progress in meeting goals and to help identify any necessary changes.

A. **Performance data** is collected and evaluated for different groups of students, such as racial/ethnic groups, high and low mobility students, English as a Second Language/English Language Learners, and students in special programs including gifted, special education, or Reading Recovery.

> EXAMPLE: Students who had been at the school for three years or more were excelling. Students who were new to the school were struggling. More reading and writing information was collected on incoming students. This led to better transitional instruction and resulted in substantial gains.

B. **Student data** are collected and evaluated, including retention numbers, participation in school programs, discipline data, assessment data, attendance data, and attitude data.

> EXAMPLE: Several intermediate students were struggling academically and behaviorally. When the data were collected, it was determined that 25% of these students had been retained. Self-esteem activities and academic interventions were expanded. Students' academic performance and behavior improved considerably.

C. **Teacher data** are collected and analyzed for staff development, training, experience, and turnover rate.

D. **Information on indicators of literacy success is collected and evaluated,** including student performance data, surveys, standardized test data, standards data, number of students leaving Title I and other programs, and reading and writing performance data.

> EXAMPLE: After analyzing data, the staff discovered students in Grades 3 through 6 were more successful when reading narrative materials but had greater difficulty with content area materials. The staff emphasized nonfiction reading strategies, and student performance improved significantly.

E. **Materials information** is collected regarding the availability of reading and writing materials, supplemental reading materials, and library materials.

> EXAMPLE: Library data were evaluated to see if there were enough high-interest, low-reading-level materials. Based on this information, more high-interest, low-level books and magazines were added to the library collection.

F. **Program data** are collected, including types of programs available, number of students reached, effectiveness of each, and cost.

> EXAMPLE: Students leaving Reading Recovery were monitored. Classroom teachers felt the students were falling behind. A program was added where former Reading Recovery students received extra support once a week using classroom guided reading materials. With this small amount of extra support, these students were able to be successful in their classroom guided reading instruction.

EFFECTIVE PRACTICE 7

MAXIMIZING AVAILABLE RESOURCES
Utilization of resources reflects the literacy goals of the school.

Some areas that can be taken into consideration are as follows:

A. Personnel—The assignment of personnel reflects the goals of the building. The educators with the strongest reading and writing background should be working with struggling readers and writers.

B. Time—The schedule reflects the commitment to literacy, with long blocks of uninterrupted time being set aside for literacy instruction. Research (Taylor, Pearson, Clark, and Walpole, 2000) has found that, ideally, a minimum of 90 minutes per day is spent on reading with another 60 minutes per day being spent on writing.

C. Budget—Money is set aside for literacy purposes, including materials, libraries, staff development, and personnel.

D. Materials—Students and teachers have access to a wide variety of materials.

> TIP: Different types of reading materials on many different levels lead to greater success—books, magazines, fiction, and nonfiction.

EFFECTIVE PRACTICE 8

ABUNDANT AND FOCUSED STAFF DEVELOPMENT
There is abundant, data-driven, focused staff development on effective literacy practices.

Staff development opportunities align with the school's literacy instructional goals.

A. Abundant is defined as ideally 1-2 hours per week for whole group and another 1-2 hours per week for small groups.

B. Staff meetings are focused on improving instruction. Announcements are primarily done in other ways, such as through bulletins or email.

C. Staff development occurs in many different formats or delivery models.

> TIP: Team planning times, grade level meetings, release time, after-school meetings, peer coaching, study groups, brown bag lunch discussions, mentors, school-site visitations, or summer workshops can be used for staff development.

D. Staff development is designed for various size groups. It can be for the whole group, small groups, or individuals, based on the identified needs.

SUGGESTIONS FOR STAFF DEVELOPMENT

- Staff members can identify their individual goals. When staff members apply for staff development training, it can be decided if the request aligns with their individual goals or the building goals.

- Principals and staff members can identify staff development needs for the staff as a whole with no more than three to five goals for the year. Some of these goals may continue for several years, recognizing that it generally takes three years for change to occur.

- If a consultant is going to be brought into a building for staff development, it is effective to have a small group of staff members make the decision as to whether this is someone the entire staff should hear.

- When sending teachers for staff training, one elementary school found greater success by sending two teachers—a primary teacher and an intermediate teacher. This led to more sharing of information as well as developed more staff camaraderie.

E. Funding should reflect the value attached to staff development.

Staff development will have the maximum value when:

- It links to building and individual goals.
- The principal is a participant.
- There is cross-grade-level articulation or planning regarding implementation.
- It is continuous and ongoing.
- There is follow-up, including observations focusing on the staff development topic/s.
- There is buy-in by staff members.
- Staff see the value in what they are doing, which means there is ongoing evaluation that demonstrates the impact of the staff development.

EFFECTIVE PRACTICE 9

STRONG FAMILY AND COMMUNITY INVOLVEMENT
Parents, families, and community are highly involved.

A. Parent communication is ongoing and frequent, focusing on individual students, curriculum, instruction, and staff development.

EXAMPLE: Teachers communicated with parents weekly using postcards, phone calls, notes, classroom newsletters, and email. A major focus was on "good news." This led to stronger family involvement and support.

B. There are many different ways of involving families in literacy activities.

> EXAMPLE: A family literacy night became a yearly event. There were many different kinds of literacy activities, including read alouds by district personnel, storytelling activities, author visits, and student sharing of writing. These events led to stronger parental interest in literacy.

C. Volunteering opportunities are wide and varied.

> TIP: Identify and utilize the unique talents of family members.
>
> EXAMPLE: Bilingual parents were asked to teach words in their native language and teach about their culture. Their participation in school literacy activities increased.
>
> TIP: Create at-home projects for those parents unable to come to school, such as tape recording books and content area materials.

D. Families are involved in schoolwide decision making by having them participate in a variety of ways, such as site councils, district committees, and advocacy groups.

E. Community members are involved in the school through partnerships, senior citizen activities, school alumni activities, recreational activities, and other civic activities.

EFFECTIVE PRACTICE 10

EMBEDDING CHANGE AND SEEKING CONTINUOUS IMPROVEMENT

Change becomes a part of the school culture and continuous improvement is an ongoing goal.

Often schools change their focus or goals prior to the changes becoming embedded.

> TIP: It takes a minimum of three years for any changes to become a permanent part of the school's literacy program. It is critical that enough time be allowed to ensure that the changes do not disappear and that educators do not revert back to the way they have always done things.

A. Change requires trust and a risk-taking environment.

B. The change process is never done—it is important that continuous improvement be seen as an ongoing part of a school's culture.

FIRST AND LASTING IMPRESSIONS
A Survey for Schools

Schools achieve greater academic success when everyone takes pride in the school. Therefore, it can be valuable to have different people visit the school or classrooms and evaluate them on the following criteria:

As you **approach the school**, what do you notice?

- ❑ Neighborhood
- ❑ Parking lot—available parking identified
- ❑ General appearance of the building
- ❑ Exterior including paint, brickwork, sidewalks, roof, graffiti
- ❑ Cleanliness and attractiveness of building and grounds
- ❑ Handicapped parking and access
- ❑ Reader board with current information
- ❑ Clearly identified entrance to office

As you **enter the building**, what do you notice?

- ❑ Directional signs
- ❑ Map of school with "You Are Here" indicated

As you **enter the office**, what do you notice?

- ❑ Home-type atmosphere with couch, bookcase with reading materials for adults and children, lighting other than florescent, softness, color, rugs, and so on.
- ❑ Bulletin boards focusing on building and district goals
- ❑ Showcasing of student work
- ❑ Office is physically approachable—visually pleasant, counters that can be seen over, easy to see who should be approached
- ❑ Wall calendar of events
- ❑ Clear directions for visitors
- ❑ Names and/or photos of staff members available
- ❑ Manner in which phones are answered

As you **view the halls**, what do you notice?

- ❑ Space is used to focus on students and learning
- ❑ Lighting and use of color
- ❑ Lack of clutter

Copyright © 2004 by Corwin Press. All rights reserved. Reprinted from *The Book of Reading and Writing Ideas, Tips, and Lists for the Elementary Classroom* by Sandra E. Anderson. Thousand Oaks, CA: Corwin Press, www.corwinpress.com. Reproduction authorized only for the local school site that has purchased this book.

❏ Signs identifying room number, teacher's name, and grade level

❏ Restrooms clearly identified for adults and children

❏ A feeling of safety and security

As you **approach the staff** at the school, what do you notice?

❏ Friendly, smiling faces

❏ Greeting and inquiry as to what can be done to help you

❏ Positive attitudes, upbeat feeling, good energy, humor, laughter

❏ Adults responding to students, students responding to adults

When you **look in the classrooms**, what do you notice?

❏ Focus of classroom is on learning

❏ Attractiveness of the classroom

❏ Clear instructional goals and behavior expectations posted

❏ Cleanliness and orderliness of the classroom

❏ Soft places for students to sit and/or read

❏ Appropriate furniture for the age of students

❏ Places where students can work independently and/or quietly

❏ Technology available for student use

❏ Quantity of literacy materials

❏ Student work showcased

❏ Student-created bulletin boards

❏ Environment that supports learning

❏ If viewing the room from the height of the students, what do you see?

When you **view the library**, what do you notice?

❏ Students using the facility

❏ The quantity and quality of reading materials

❏ The organization of the room

❏ The lighting of the library

❏ Furniture appropriate for the ages of the students

❏ The enthusiasm of the librarian and any helpers

❏ Organization of books—books can be reached by students and many covers are visible

❏ Check-out procedures—students are not limited in number of books they can check-out, and they can visit the library frequently

Copyright © 2004 by Corwin Press. All rights reserved. Reprinted from *The Book of Reading and Writing Ideas, Tips, and Lists for the Elementary Classroom* by Sandra E. Anderson. Thousand Oaks, CA: Corwin Press, www.corwinpress.com. Reproduction authorized only for the local school site that has purchased this book.

Evaluation Checklist for Effective Schools and Effective Classrooms

Effective literacy practices will be far more successful if a school has implemented effective school and effective classroom research. Those schools that incorporate what we know about effective schools, effective teachers, and effective literacy practices will see dramatic results.

Rate each item on a 1-4 scale.	Low			High
1. Our school is student-centered with high expectations for all students.	1	2	3	4
2. There is a shared purpose with a focus on literacy.	1	2	3	4
3. We have strong instructional leadership with frequent monitoring of teaching and learning.	1	2	3	4
4. Staff members utilize effective classroom practices.	1	2	3	4
5. There is alignment of curriculum, instruction, and assessment.	1	2	3	4
6. There is an abundance of high-quality materials.	1	2	3	4
7. Data and information are routinely collected and used when making literacy decisions.	1	2	3	4
8. The use of available resources reflects our focus on literacy instruction.	1	2	3	4
9. Staff development is focused on literacy and is ongoing.	1	2	3	4
10. Families and community are highly involved.	1	2	3	4
11. Continuous improvement is an ongoing goal.	1	2	3	4
12. We are a strong, caring staff.	1	2	3	4
13. Students have a strong sense of belonging.	1	2	3	4
14. Classroom management and organization are excellent.	1	2	3	4
15. Knowledge of effective literacy practices is outstanding.	1	2	3	4
16. Instructional skills are strong.	1	2	3	4

SCORING: Any area scoring below a 3 needs to be evaluated in greater depth. It is essential that effective school and effective classroom practices be in place if a school is to excel in reading and writing.

Copyright © 2004 by Corwin Press. All rights reserved. Reprinted from *The Book of Reading and Writing Ideas, Tips, and Lists for the Elementary Classroom* by Sandra E. Anderson. Thousand Oaks, CA: Corwin Press, www.corwinpress.com. Reproduction authorized only for the local school site that has purchased this book.

Chapter 2
Components of an Effective, Complete Reading Program

Success Story

A group of intermediate students did not want to read during independent reading. The teacher posted a chart to record who was reading. Students started reading with no rewards or incentives, just an X on the chart. After a month of reading, students requested a reward for reading. When asked what they would like, they suggested that any student reading 20 minutes every day for 30 days should receive a book of their choice from the classroom library autographed by the teacher. It was at this point that the teacher realized most of these students had never owned a book of their own. In addition, students started self-selecting to read.

There are six components of an effective, complete reading program. Each of these is critical in strengthening students' reading. If all six components are present, students' literacy growth will be enhanced.

Read Aloud provides teachers with an opportunity to model reading and to expose students to higher-level materials.

Shared Reading provides support for readers as they read along with the teacher.

Guided Reading is small, flexible group instruction that allows the teacher to tailor instruction to the needs of a particular group of students.

Literacy Centers and Literature Circles provide students with opportunities to practice and apply the skills and strategies they have learned in guided reading.

Independent Reading encourages students to read on their own and to develop a love of reading.

COMPONENT 1

READ ALOUD

Definition: A teacher reads a challenging, high-interest text to a group of students.

Why read aloud?

1. Reading aloud models fluent reading and allows the teacher to model specific strategies that will be taught later in shared and guided reading.

2. Reading aloud demonstrates to students that there are more interesting, enticing materials than what they are reading at their instructional level.

3. Reading aloud develops listening skills, builds language skills, enhances vocabulary, positively impacts fluency, strengthens reading comprehension, and improves attitudes towards reading.

4. Reading aloud improves students' reading and writing performance and increases their desire to read.

What does reading aloud look like?

1. The teacher makes the reading interactive through activities such as discussing the author's style, using questioning strategies, or retelling parts of the reading.

    TIP: To maximize instructional time, the skills that are being taught during reading and writing instruction can be highlighted during read aloud.

2. If the teacher's purpose of the read aloud is to model "good reader" strategies, the teacher periodically points out the strategies that he or she is using.

3. If the teacher's purpose of the read aloud is for students to enjoy higher-level text (at students' listening levels or approximately 2 years above reading levels), the teacher may focus on the content, vocabulary, or language structures.

    TIP: Students need to hear great language and be encouraged to play with language. Read aloud is a perfect place to share the "joy of language."

    RESOURCE: Jim Trelease's *Read Aloud Handbook*, 5th edition (2001) is an outstanding source of read aloud titles as well as research on reading aloud.

What does reading aloud NOT look like?

1. Students are not interested or engaged in what is being read.

2. Students are drawing, writing, or walking around.

3. The teacher is not enjoying the book or selection.

4. The teacher continues a book that is not being enjoyed, that does not read aloud well, or that is too difficult for the students to comprehend.

What materials should be used?

1. If the purpose is strategy introduction, the read aloud should be high-quality literature,

age appropriate, and suitable for the particular strategy being presented. For example, if sequencing is the skill being introduced, then the selection should be a text where sequencing is important.

2. The book or selection must be of high interest and suitable for reading aloud. Not all books or selections read aloud well.

3. A wide range of materials should be used…fiction, nonfiction, many different genres.

> TIP: This is wonderful time for the teacher to share a favorite selection—poetry, nonfiction, a humorous story, or whatever is important to the teacher. Students benefit from listening to adults who enjoy reading.

What do we know about reading aloud?

1. Children who come to school with low language skills or limited experience with being read to should be read to four to seven times per day. Some reading aloud can be done one-on-one or in small groups by trained volunteers. This is critical to reading success because…

   • This is where children learn story structure and text structures.

   • This is where children learn how written language differs from oral language.

   • This is where an appreciation of reading and language can develop.

   • This is where students can be introduced to new concepts, new vocabulary, interesting words, and different writing structures.

2. All children benefit from being read aloud to because they are able to listen to stories that are beyond their reading level. Reading aloud leads to superior gains in reading comprehension and vocabulary development.

3. All classrooms benefit from reading aloud because it builds a community of learners based around a common text.

> RESOURCES: *The Power of Reading: Insights From the Research* by Krashen, *The Art of Teaching Reading* by Calkins, *Becoming a Nation of Readers* by National Academy of Education, and "Project Story Boost: Read Alouds for Students at Risk" by Wood and Salvetti.

Read Aloud Innovations

1. Develop grade-level recommended titles (particularly chapter books).

   > EXAMPLE: Put up a chart listing different genres and have staff members fill in their favorite read alouds. Evaluate titles as to grade-level appropriateness and negotiate best titles for each grade. Add on to the list over time. This eliminates overlap and encourages teachers to read new titles.

   > TIP: Develop favorite read aloud lists by having students provide their favorite titles. Keep in mind that read aloud selections should generally be 2 years above the average instructional reading level.

2. Use a wide variety of materials for read aloud including poetry, newspaper articles, and magazine articles.

3. Encourage local day cares and preschools to read aloud.

    TIPS: Students can collect preschool-level books to donate to the local preschools and day cares. In addition, teachers can establish visitation days when preschoolers visit the classroom for cross-age story times. Another option is for students to encourage the school librarian or local bookstores to have preschool story times. The benefits of increasing read aloud time for preschoolers are enormous.

4. Provide parents with recommended read aloud lists and establish a lending library of read alouds.

5. Invite guest readers to read aloud to students.

    TIP: Invite the principal, superintendent, community members, school board members, and parents to read aloud to students.

COMPONENT 2

SHARED READING

Definition: The whole class gathers to read and discuss a text that has been enlarged. Students participate in a choral reading of the text and follow-up discussion.

Why include shared reading?

1. It models the reading process with carefully selected material while actively engaging students in the reading process.

2. It allows teachers to focus on particular features including concepts of print, rhyme, and repetition.

3. It provides an opportunity for the teacher to teach specific reading skills and strategies including phonics, sight vocabulary, syntax, and comprehension.

4. All students experience success. Students who read at lower levels have opportunities to participate and to hear fluent reading.

What does shared reading look like?

1. At the primary level, the teacher uses an enlarged text of carefully selected material, taking into consideration the concepts, the vocabulary, the sentence structure, the length of the book, and the size of the print.

    TIP: The shared reading lesson will typically be 10-30 minutes depending upon the length of the book, the skills being taught, and the students' attention span.

    TIP: Nonfiction big books are readily available and provide opportunities for the teacher to introduce nonfiction text formats. Also, this meets the needs of those students more interested in nonfiction topics.

2. The teacher introduces the book and invites students to predict what the story will be about. The teacher builds on students' prior knowledge or, if necessary, builds essential background knowledge. The teacher then begins reading and encourages students to join in as they are comfortable. Often students will initially join in on the repetitive phrases. At the conclusion of the reading there will be a response to the story.

> TIP: If the teacher develops students' background knowledge prior to reading, the students will be able to comprehend material that is more difficult and more complex.

> EXAMPLE: When the shared book was about the solar system, the teacher took a few minutes to assess what students already knew about the solar system. In addition, the teacher had students look at the illustrations and predict the content of the book.

3. The teacher uses shared reading to assess students' knowledge of print and to plan future instruction. Some areas to evaluate include students' understanding that print carries a message, directionality, and sense of story.

> TIP: Any identified areas needing more instruction can be a focus of future shared reading lessons. To reinforce this instruction, the same topics can be a part of modeled writing.

4. The shared reading text will be reread with different concepts being addressed each time the text is read. The teacher will select the teaching concepts based on students' needs.

> RESOURCE: Bobbi Fisher and Emily Fisher Medvic's *Perspectives on Shared Reading: Planning and Practice* (2000).

5. At the intermediate level, shared reading can be used to develop skills and fluency. Teachers may enlarge a piece of text to use on an overhead projector or on wall charts. Students may read different sections based on the skill being taught...dialogue, character parts, setting, descriptions, or content.

> TIP: Mini-lessons of 10-15 minutes work well for introducing new genres, for teaching nonfiction text format, or for working on fluency.

> TIP: Shared reading is a great way to teach dialogue where the speaker is not identified. The students can be grouped by characters and then can read the lines. This helps students see which character is speaking.

What does shared reading NOT look like?
1. The teacher is doing all the reading.
2. Students are inattentive.
3. Too many skills are being taught.
4. The repeated readings of the book seem like agony.
5. The schedule is rigid—one book for an entire week no matter what.

What materials should be used?

1. Books should be selected to align to students' needs. The reading level should be near the reading level of the middle of the group. The books should also focus on the skills or strategies that are being taught. The text should be large enough so that all students can easily see the text. At the emergent level the text should be predictable with a repetitive pattern.

    TIP: Class-made big books are great shared reading materials. Students enjoy reading the books they have created.

2. Materials can be big books, wall stories, pocket chart materials, song charts, chants, or any other enlarged text.

    TIP: Poems and other single-page materials can be enlarged to chart size. These are wonderful sources for single copies of shared reading materials.

3. Other materials that are helpful for the teacher include highlighter tape, sticky notes, and word frames.

    TIP: Highlighter tape can be placed over certain words. This focuses students on specific words for vocabulary or phonics instruction. Sticky notes can cover word endings so that students can "figure out" the word ending or they can cover an entire word and students can use the context to "predict" the word. Word frames are great for students who are having difficulty identifying individual words. The teacher or students can place the frame around one specific word.

What we know about shared reading?

1. Shared reading builds success for all readers but is particularly valuable for struggling readers.

2. Shared reading is one of the best ways to enhance fluency.

3. Shared reading is controlled by the teacher, with the lesson specifically designed to meet students' needs.

4. Shared reading can be done with a wide variety of materials.

5. Shared reading provides an opportunity to teach skills and strategies in context.

6. Shared reading is one way of modeling literary discussions.

Shared Reading Innovations

1. Look creatively at options for materials. Wall stories, pocket charts, poem charts, chants, jump rope jingles, children's magazines, and content area materials are wonderful resources.

    TIP: When students create pages for class books, create a wall story by posting the pages in the classroom prior to putting them into a class book. These can be used for shared reading. When they are taken down, they can be put into a class book. (Wood-Walters, 1999).

2. Develop a grid listing the skills that need to be taught on one side of the grid and the shared reading materials on the other axis. Check which skills can be taught with which materials. When purchasing new materials, select those materials that will best complete the grid.

    TIP: The grid makes it easier to select the book that will best meet students' needs at any particular point in time.

3. Use shared reading time to reinforce skill instruction.

    EXAMPLE: The following were identified as skills to be taught during shared reading.

    Concepts of Print—top to bottom, left to right, return sweep, one-to-one correspondence, concept of word or phrase

    Word Study—phonics skills, onsets and rimes, word wall additions, high-frequency words, word choice

    Grammar and Conventions—capitalization and punctuation, verb tense, pronouns, sentence structure

    Content—beginning, middle, and end, logical organization, main idea, voice, genre, format

4. Use a large envelope for each shared reading selection. List the skills that can be taught on the outside of the envelope. Any supplies such as sentence strips, picture cards, or word cards can be kept in the envelope and attached to the big book.

    TIP: Shared reading activities can be moved to a literacy center to provide additional practice with known material.

5. Create generic activities that can be used many different times with little preparation.

    TIP: Graphic organizers for story maps and nonfiction text structures can be enlarged, laminated, and used over and over again with different shared reading materials.

6. Use shared reading materials for word study.

    TIP: Cover a word and have students predict the word by uncovering the first letter. This works well with higher-performing students because they can predict more complex vocabulary choices. Then uncover the word letter by letter and have students revise their predictions. Talk about which of their predictions could be correct and why.

7. Make shared reading materials available as a part of the print-rich classroom environment or as a part of a literacy center.

    TIP: Limit the number of shared reading materials available to students during center time. If too many options are available, students may have difficulty staying focused.

8. Invite other teachers to be guest readers for shared reading. This allows the classroom teacher to observe his/her students during the shared reading time.

COMPONENT 3

GUIDED READING

Definition: Small, flexible groups of students, at approximately the same reading level, read the same new instructional-level text that has been selected by the teacher.

The lesson is designed by the teacher to meet the needs of the students in this particular group. The teacher observes, coaches, prompts, and evaluates students. Each student reads his/her own copy of the book at his/her own pace while the teacher monitors each student by listening to the student read a portion of the text.

Generally, the size of the group is between 4 and 6. Flexible means that students move up or down groups dependent upon their need, with group membership being reassessed at least once every 4-6 weeks. Instructional level is defined as material where students can accurately decode 90-94% of the words and comprehend what is being read.

Why do guided reading?

1. Students become better readers by practicing reading in "just right" material where they are experiencing success.

2. All students need instruction to improve their reading.

    TIP: High-achieving students need guided reading to advance in their reading performance. The skills become more sophisticated and may include such skills as foreshadowing, figurative language, and vocabulary choice.

3. Teachers can better identify students' needs by working with individuals within small groups of students. Teachers can provide support, guidance, demonstrations, or explanations as necessary.

4. Small groups allow students to learn from one another through meaningful, focused discussions.

5. Students will learn how to use "good reader" strategies and solve problems as they read new text independently.

What does guided reading look like?

1. Small, flexible groups of 4-6 children gather around the teacher to read an instructional-level text selected specifically for this group of students.

2. The teacher will work with the small group for 15-30 minutes.

3. The lesson is structured to include warm-up or familiar reading, pre-reading, during-reading, and after-reading activities based on students' needs.

4. Familiar reading provides an opportunity for students to reread familiar books from previous guided reading lessons. Familiar reading enhances decoding, comprehension, and fluency.

5. Pre-reading activities are short and are carefully chosen to help students achieve greater success. The pre-reading activities selected by the teacher will vary according to the text

and the needs of the students. Emergent readers need more time spent on pre-reading activities to ensure that they can be successful.

> TIP: These may include assessing students' prior knowledge, providing a summary statement, developing necessary background knowledge, building personal connections, incorporating engagement- or interest-generating activities, predicting content, or presenting critical words.

> EXAMPLE: The teacher selects a book about different kinds of frogs and provides a summary statement about the book. Then the teacher asks students what they know about frogs and has students preview the book. Students are asked to find several high-frequency words to ensure that they know these words. The teacher engages students in the material by asking them to look for information about unusual frogs.

6. Students individually read the text at their own pace, keeping the goal or purpose in mind as they read. The teacher "leans in" to listen to samples of each child's reading and provides prompts, questions, or responses based on individual students' needs.

> TIP: A staggered start, where teachers have each student start at a slightly different time, ensures that each student is doing his/her own reading.

> TIP: The teacher can use this time to take running records, to write anecdotal notes, and to collect ongoing assessment information.

> TIP: Listening to the students read will provide ideas for follow-up activities. If students struggle with a particular word or concept, this can be the focus of the follow-up.

7. Students continue to read even if rereading is required.

> TIP: Students are using the "never done" strategy—they keep reading until the teacher has had a chance to listen to all of the students. This helps to build fluency.

8. The teacher concludes each guided reading lesson by using a follow-up or an after-reading strategy that either links back to the pre-reading strategy, reinforces the goals and purposes, or provides a follow-up or extension activity. After-reading strategies provide focused instruction based on teacher observations to enhance comprehension, to reinforce skills, or to connect to students' lives.

> TIP: Follow-up activities should take less time than the actual reading. Most of students' guided reading time should be spent reading. Often the extension activities can be completed during independent work time.

9. The other students (those not in this guided reading group) are involved in meaningful literacy activities during the guided reading lessons. These could include literacy centers, meaningful independent work, literature circle activities, or reading/writing activities.

> RESOURCES: *Guided Reading: Good First Teaching for All Children (1996)* and *Guiding Reading and Writers, Grades 3-6* (2001) by Fountas and Pinnell.

What does guided reading NOT look like?

1. Whole group instruction
2. Round robin reading where students listen to each other reading while waiting their turn.

3. The teacher is away from the guided reading group.

4. The teacher is frequently interrupted or involved with other students.

5. Students are "going through the motions."

6. Teachers are reading the text to students.

What materials should be used?

1. Sets of leveled reading books on students' instructional levels. This requires many books. Emergent readers should be reading a new book every day. Developing and fluent readers may read continuing books such as chapter books.

   TIP: Ideally a school should have 200 sets of different titles for kindergarten and Grade 1 and 100 sets of titles for each of the other grade levels. Generally a set consists of six books because the guided reading group is limited to six or fewer students. These can be built up over time.

2. Books should reflect a wide variety of genres including nonfiction.

   TIP: When students are at the fluent level, content area materials may be used for guided reading instruction.

3. Other valuable guided reading materials include white boards, chalkboards, sticky notes, and highlighter tape.

   TIP: Individual white boards or chalkboards can be used for word practice. This is particularly effective for practicing vocabulary found in the guided reading books.

What do we know about guided reading?

1. The only way for students to improve in reading is by reading material on their instructional levels.

2. Group membership should be flexible, with students moving between groups. A reevaluation of group placement should occur at least once every 4-6 weeks.

3. To incorporate guided reading groups, excellent management skills and organizational procedures must be in place. Students must be taught these procedures.

4. Teacher-designed lessons can better meet students' needs because teachers know their students' instructional levels and can tailor instruction to better meet their students' needs.

5. Ongoing assessment is critical for group adjustments and for planning instruction.

6. Students' risk taking and engagement increase dramatically during small group guided reading instruction.

Guided Reading Innovations

1. If a teacher has more than six students reading at one particular level, then the group can be split into two groups so that students can be individually monitored.

   TIP: Guided reading groups can be taught by paraprofessionals or other support personnel. However, it is important that these groups rotate to the classroom teacher so that teachers know each of their students' reading levels. Often the most struggling readers work with the least trained personnel—it should be the opposite, the most struggling readers need the best trained literacy teachers.

2. Leveled books can be organized in a wide variety of ways.

TIP: Teachers can level books by sorting books into three categories—easy, more difficult, and hard. These three piles can then be resorted to create nine levels of books. In addition, there are many lists available for leveled books.

RESOURCE: *Matching Books to Readers: Using Leveled Books in Guided Reading K-3* (1999) by Fountas and Pinnell.

TIP: One school district created book rooms for leveled books. The books were labeled and numbered with sticky-dots for the appropriate grade level. The numbers 1-199 were used for kindergarten and Grade 1 books with the easier books having lower numbers 1-50, the middle difficulty having numbers 51-120, and the more difficult having numbers 121-199. Grade 2 materials were numbered from 200-299 with easier 200-230, middle 231-260, and harder 261-299. Other grades were numbered accordingly. You can start with fewer titles and then add as necessary or when funding becomes available.

COMPONENT 4

LITERACY CENTERS

Definition: Literacy centers consist of independent, multi-leveled activities where students rotate through the centers or self-select the center of their choice.

One of the most frequently asked questions is, "What do I do with the other students while I'm teaching guided reading?" Literacy centers can provide students with multiple opportunities to practice and apply what they have been taught during guided reading.

Why incorporate literacy centers?

1. Students have opportunities to practice and apply their literacy skills.
2. Students can work on multi-leveled materials that meet their individual needs.
3. Students can explore and investigate different curriculum areas.
4. Students learn to collaborate and to take responsibility for their work.
5. Teachers can work with small, flexible guided reading groups.

What do literacy centers look like?

1. Students are engaged in a variety of literacy activities.
2. The literacy centers are spread around the room, maximizing the use of available classroom space.

3. Teachers teach classroom rules and procedures for using literacy centers.

> TIP: Start with only one or two centers. Then add additional centers. Reteach procedures after vacations or when new students enter the classroom.

4. Teachers model literacy center activities prior to expecting students to complete the activities.

5. There is a management system in place.

> TIP: A rotation system has students rotate through the centers in a prescribed order. A self-selection system allows students to make choices. In either system, it is important to limit the number of students who can be at a center at any one time and to provide clear directions for center activities.

6. Literacy center activities are meaningful and students are held accountable for literacy center work.

> TIP: Each literacy center can include multi-leveled activities or multi-leveled materials to meet students' needs. This is one way of meeting the needs of high-achieving students as well as providing practice for struggling readers.

> EXAMPLE: All students can be looking for multi-syllabic words, but can use different materials at different reading levels. Or, all students can be writing letters, but the sophistication of the letter could vary according to each student's writing ability.

What do literacy centers NOT look like?

1. Disorganized, chaotic, or out of control.
2. Students unclear about what they should be doing.
3. All students doing exactly the same activities.

What materials should be used?

1. Any relevant materials, including reading and writing activities, literacy games, or word practice activities. The key is that the materials provide students with meaningful practice opportunities.

> TIP: Literacy centers are a great place to use supplemental materials and content area materials.

2. Guided reading and shared reading materials can be a part of literacy center activities.

> RESOURCE: *The Complete Guide to Classroom Centers* (1996) by Linda Holliman.

What do we know about literacy centers?

1. Students benefit from opportunities to practice and apply literacy skills.
2. Students enjoy having choices and behavior problems often diminish.
3. Science and social studies activities can become part of literacy centers.
4. Literacy centers are one way of differentiating instruction to meet diverse students needs.

Literacy Center Innovations

1. **Reading Center**—The classroom library can be a center. A wide variety of materials can be available, including wordless books, alphabet books, counting books, nursery rhymes, fairy tales, picture books, magazines, or chapter books. Books can be organized by book levels, genres, or themes.

2. **Reading the Room/Writing the Room**—Students can use the print-rich environment as a center. This can be done individually or with partners. To be more accountable, students can record specific things they have read using a clipboard and recording sheet.

3. **Shared Books**—The big books and other shared reading materials can become a center. Pocket chart activities based on shared books can be particularly effective practice activities.

4. **Poem Charts**—Poems that have been taught in class can be hung on chart racks for students to read.

5. **Jokes & Riddles Center**—Joke books and riddle books can be made available. Students can collect their favorite jokes and riddles or create their own.

6. **Overhead Projector Center**—Familiar text can put on overhead transparencies and students can read and illustrate the text. They can also look for particular words, such as adjectives or descriptive words.

7. **ABC Center**—ABC books can be a center with activities focusing on letter-sound relationships. This is a great way to build vocabulary along with knowledge of letters and sounds. Books, materials, and manipulatives can be changed periodically.

   TIP: This center can be particularly effective with fluent and high-achieving readers by using more sophisticated materials. *Albert B. Cub and Zebra* (1977) by Rockwell is great for vocabulary development and *A My Name Is Alice* (1992) by Bayer and Kellogg is wonderful for alliteration and geography.

8. **Word Center**—Students can study words at the appropriate level. The words can be taken from the books they are reading during guided reading, from their writing, or any other curriculum area.

   TIP: The word wall can be utilized for center activities, including creating new words using the words on the word wall or creating multi-syllabic words.

   TIP: Standardized test formats can be practiced in this center—identifying synonyms, antonyms, vocabulary, and so on.

9. **Sequencing Center**—Students can sequence sentence strips of the story they have read during guided reading. Students can match text to pictures or sequence only the text. The activity level should align to the student's reading level.

   TIP: Poems can be used. Students enjoy reading their "silly" sequences. Also, one student can write the sentence strips to be sequenced and then another student can do the sequencing.

10. **Writing Center**—Students can use a wide variety of materials and can be given a specific writing task or an open-ended task.

> TIP: Multi-leveled activities are easy to create—students can choose from a menu of options. Options can include writing their own pattern book by creating an innovation of an existing pattern book; writing a new story based on a literature model; creating a nonfiction information poster; or selecting five vocabulary words from a container and then writing a story that includes the five words.

> TIP: Journal writing can be a part of the Writing Center. Students may write to the teacher, write responses to things they have read, or answer questions posed by the teacher.

> TIP: Spelling and publishing centers can be a part of the Writing Center.

11. **Listening Center**—Students can listen to prepared tapes or make their own taped copies of the stories they are reading.

> TIP: Tapes can be made by guest readers. Students love to listen to the principal or other staff members.

> TIP: Students can record stories for younger students.

12. **Research Center**—Students can research different content area topics. They can also write about these topics.

> TIP: This is a great way to incorporate social studies or science resources and activities.

> TIP: The Research Center is a wonderful way of challenging high-achieving students.

13. **Real-Life Literacy Kits**—Teachers and students collect items around a particular real-life theme.

> EXAMPLE: One of these could be restaurant information, including menus, phone book pages listing restaurants, restaurant reviews, lists of supplies, and order forms. Students can then participate in a variety of activities such as ordering a meal with a limited amount of money or writing a restaurant review.

14. **Computer Center**—The computer can be a motivating literacy center where students can practice and apply reading and writing skills.

15. **Art Center**—An art center can be used to reinforce literacy skills. Students can illustrate text they have read, draw pictures of characters, or create posters of information. However, it is critical that the activities enhance students' literacy skills.

COMPONENT 5

LITERATURE CIRCLES

Definition: Students select a text from options provided by the teacher. Small groups of students then read and discuss the text in depth. The teacher will generally be a part of the group as a facilitator or observer. Literature circles are used primarily with fluent readers.

Why use literature circles?

1. Students are motivated and challenged to read.
2. Discussions promote higher-level thinking and a community of learners.
3. Students demonstrate more interest in reading because of the social aspect of literature circles.
4. Literature circles provide a perfect opportunity for students to practice and apply their reading and writing skills.
5. Literature circles lead to enhanced student performance.
6. Students become more responsible for their own learning.
7. Students can be flexibly grouped.

What do literature circles look like?

1. Students are grouped by book selections.
2. The literature circle activities and procedures are taught.
3. Reading is purposeful with students highly involved in independently reading the text.
4. Students complete response journals, answer pre-determined questions, complete graphic organizers, or finish other activities prior to meeting for discussions.
5. Students meet frequently and discuss the section of the book they have read.
6. Students will lead the groups with the teacher's role varying from participant to observer depending upon the needs of the group.

    TIP: As students gain experience with literature circles, the teacher may only occasionally participate in the group.

7. Students are held accountable for all work and can be involved in self-assessment.
8. Students may be assigned follow-up or presentation activities.

What do literature circles NOT look like?

1. All students are reading the same book.
2. Students are not reading and discussing the book.
3. Students are not purposeful in their discussions.

What materials should be used?

1. There will be sets of books, and each student will have his/her own copy of the literature circle book. These books will be on students' instructional or independent reading levels. The number of books needed will be determined by the size of the literature circle group, the length of the books, and how often students participate in literature circles.

    TIP: Limit the size of the group to six or fewer students to promote discussion and involvement by all students.

    RESOURCES: *Getting Started With Literature Circles* (1999) by Noe, Johnson and Hill or *Literature Circles: Voices and Choice in the Student-Centered Classroom* (1994) by Daniels.

2. Many different genres can be used.

    TIP: Link literature circle choices to content areas being studied. For example, if the environment is an area of study, then the literature circle choices could include fiction and nonfiction books about the environment.

3. Other necessary materials include response journals and sticky notes.

What do we know about literature circles?

1. Students become more reflective readers.

2. Students enjoy being a member of a "book club."

3. Discussions enhance reading comprehension.

Literature Circle Innovations

1. All students can read selections around a central classroom theme, but titles can be on different reading levels.

    EXAMPLE: The class was studying the Civil War. The teacher selected five different titles relating to the Civil War. Less capable readers chose from the lower-level titles, more capable from the higher-level titles.

2. Teachers can post charts of pre-reading, during-reading, and after-reading strategies in the classroom so that literature circle groups can be reminded to use these strategies.

    TIP: As students participate in literature circles, they can identify which reading strategies they found most helpful. This promotes the transfer of these strategies to students' independent reading.

3. The procedures can be modeled and practiced. This leads to more on-task behaviors during literature circles.

    EXAMPLE: A fishbowl strategy can be utilized. This is where one group sits in the center and conducts their literature circle. The other students sit around the perimeter as observers. At the end, the group in the center discusses how they felt it went, the group around the perimeter gives positive comments, suggestions, and asks questions about what occurred.

4. Literature circle response journal entries can be aligned to state standards.

    TIP: If persuasive writing is a district or state standard, then the response journal entries can link the literature circle activities to this particular type of writing.

5. Literature circle activities can be aligned to identified student needs.

    TIP: If vocabulary is a concern, then literature circles activities can focus on vocabulary, word choice, and interesting words.

6. Students may be assigned roles much like cooperative learning roles.

7. English as a Second Language and English Language Learners can read books in two languages—in their first language and in English.

    TIP: This is a great way to involve bilingual parents or community members. They can record the books in both languages.

8. Teachers can form their own book clubs for adult leisure reading. Students like hearing about teachers' literature circles.

COMPONENT 6

INDEPENDENT READING

Definition: Students read independently in self-selected materials for pleasure. The teacher's role is to read, monitor, observe, acknowledge, or respond to students.

Why incorporate independent reading?

1. Independent reading provides opportunities for students to practice reading and apply reading strategies.

2. Independent reading improves reading performance, including comprehension, rate, and fluency.

3. Students who read more have stronger vocabularies.

4. More reading leads to improved writing, spelling, and language skills.

5. Independent reading can create a love of reading and establish an environment where students see themselves as readers.

What does independent reading look like?

1. Students are reading self-selected materials; however, because students need to be reading with 95% word recognition, teachers may occasionally assist students in book selection.

    TIP: Primary students can be taught the three-finger rule. As they read, they hold up a finger each time they come to an unknown word. If they reach three fingers on one page, the book is probably too difficult. Intermediate students can use the same strategy using five fingers.

2. Independent reading occurs every day for 10-30 minutes.

3. After independent reading, students have opportunities to discuss what they have read and share the strategies they found to be most effective.

4. Teachers read while students read.

    TIP: Independent reading will be more successful if the teacher also reads and shares something interesting from his/her reading. This can be a great time for a teacher to pre-read a future read aloud.

5. The focus is enjoyment of reading rather than instruction.

What does independent reading NOT look like?

Students are not engaged and not reading.

What materials should be used?

1. Classroom libraries of at least 300 books.

    TIP: Books can be collected in many different ways—parents can be asked to donate books to the classroom collection, garage sales are great sources of inexpensive materials, book club points can be used to add to classroom libraries, and businesses will often donate books to the classroom library.

2. Extensive school libraries.

3. Public libraries accessible to students.

What do we know about independent reading?

1. Independent reading leads to improved reading performance. Students with the highest test scores read the most pages for pleasure. The number of minutes read per day is the best predictor of reading comprehension, vocabulary size, and gains in reading achievement.

    RESOURCES: *Becoming a Nation of Readers* by National Academy of Education (1984) and *The Power of Reading* (1993) by Krashen.

2. If intermediate students were to read for 20 minutes each day, they could read more than 3,000 pages in a year—or, in the same amount of time, they could watch 8 seasons of a sit com.

Independent Reading Innovations

1. Students can keep data on their independent reading—how many minutes they have read individually, as a class, and as a school, how many pages have been read, or how many books have been read.

    TIP: Independent reading is most effective if the focus is on minutes rather than pages or number of books because students are not rewarded for selecting the easiest or shortest books.

2. Incentive programs should be used cautiously, keeping in mind why they are being used, how much time they are taking, and if they are achieving the desired results.

     TIP: The goal of independent reading is to develop a love of reading rather than reading for a prize.

3. A reading wheel can be used if you want to encourage students to read different genres.

     EXAMPLE: A wheel is divided into six sections with each section labeled with a different genre such as nonfiction, biography, fantasy, realistic fiction, mystery, and science fiction. As students read a particular genre, they color in that section or list the book in that section.

4. Students can read and develop their own "Oprah Recommended Book Lists."

     TIP: Students can take the recommended book list to a local book store or library and have them promote the books on the list.

5. Staff members can develop adult book lists and post the lists in the staff room. Students respond well when they know the staff members are also creating recommended book lists.

6. The principal can have children's books available for checkout.

7. A book swap can be organized where students trade books.

Checklist for Components of an Effective, Complete Reading Program

Rate each item on a 1-4 scale.

	Low			High
1. Read aloud occurs at all grade levels every day.	1	2	3	4
2. Shared reading is used at the primary grades.	1	2	3	4
3. Shared reading is occasionally used at the intermediate grades when fluency is an issue.	1	2	3	4
4. Guided reading or small flexible groups are used for reading instruction at all grades.	1	2	3	4
5. During guided reading, students are reading in instructional level materials (90-94% success).	1	2	3	4
6. Guided reading groups are flexible with group membership being evaluated at least once every 4-6 weeks.	1	2	3	4
7. Students are practicing and applying literacy skills in literacy centers and/or literature circles.	1	2	3	4
8. Students have 10-20 minutes every day for independent reading.	1	2	3	4
9. Primary students have guided reading every day.	1	2	3	4
10. Struggling readers have guided reading every day.	1	2	3	4
11. Intermediate students have guided reading with the teacher at least three times per week.	1	2	3	4
12. All components (read aloud, shared reading, guided reading, literacy centers or literature circles, and independent reading) are occurring in all classrooms.	1	2	3	4
13. Staff members frequently discuss reading instruction.	1	2	3	4
14. Students are visibly engaged in reading.	1	2	3	4

SCORING: Any area scoring below a 3 needs further review.

Copyright © 2004 by Corwin Press. All rights reserved. Reprinted from *The Book of Reading and Writing Ideas, Tips, and Lists for the Elementary Classroom* by Sandra E. Anderson. Thousand Oaks, CA: Corwin Press, www.corwinpress.com. Reproduction authorized only for the local school site that has purchased this book.

Chapter 3
Essential Elements of
Reading Instruction

Success Story

An elementary school decided to focus on pre-reading strategies to see if they would have an impact on students' reading performance. All staff members used a variety of pre-reading strategies. Much to their surprise, students were generally able to read material that was much more difficult—approximately one year advanced over what they had been previously reading. The value of pre-reading strategies was recognized, and pre-reading strategies became a consistent part of all reading instruction.

There are four essential elements of reading instruction—word study, language structure, fluency, and comprehension. All four are critical parts of a strong reading program.

Word study includes phonemic awareness, phonics, non-decodable or sight words, and vocabulary development.

Language Structure—An understanding of language structure or syntax is another important element of reading. Students with a good understanding of book language or written language experience greater reading success. Students who have less understanding of the language structure or syntax have more difficulty—students with low language levels, English as a Second Language students, and English Language Learners need greater language instruction.

Fluency impacts reading comprehension and students can benefit from specific instruction in fluency.

Comprehension is the goal of reading, and comprehension strategies can be taught to strengthen reading performance. Too often comprehension is assessed through follow-up questions and activities, but is not taught. It is critical that students be given strategies that will help them understand both fiction and nonfiction reading materials.

A strong reading program will teach all four essential elements.

ELEMENT 1

WORD STUDY

Phonemic Awareness

Definition: Phonemic awareness is the understanding that words are composed of a sequence of individual sounds. The phoneme is the smallest unit of sound.

Why teach phonemic awareness?

It is an important component in learning to read.

What does phonemic awareness instruction look like?

1. All activities are oral.

    TIP: Include songs, chants, word-sound games, and rhymes. Playing with sounds is the best way to strengthen phonemic awareness.

2. Activities are short—no more than 10-15 minutes of direct instruction and then reinforced throughout the day.

3. There are allowances for individual differences—children who need phonemic awareness are given many activities. Students who have already mastered phonemic awareness move on to other activities.

4. Activities are deliberate, purposeful, intentional, and based on students' needs.

5. Phonemic awareness is used in the context of real reading and writing—not in isolation.

6. Activities should be playful, engaging, and interactive.

What does phonemic awareness instruction NOT look like?

1. Activities are rigid and lengthy.

2. Phonemic awareness is rote memorization or drudgery and drill.

3. Activities are always presented to the whole group.

4. The focus is on the "sound of the week."

    RATIONALE: Teaching a sound of the week will take most of the school year to introduce the sounds. Generally students can learn 3 or more sounds a week, which means the entire alphabet can be taught in 9 weeks.

5. Focusing on nonsense words.

    RATIONALE: If students practice on nonsense words, they get better on nonsense words. The greatest benefit comes from practicing "real" words.

What materials should be used?

1. Many of the activities require no materials—teachers can use students' names, rhyming

words, and vocabulary from books being read in class.

2. Other materials could include nursery rhymes, alliteration books, or any materials that allow teachers to focus on playing with language.

> RESOURCE: *Phonemic Awareness: Playing With Sounds to Strengthen Beginning Reading Skills* (1997) by Fitzpatrick.

What do we know about phonemic awareness?

1. Lessons should move from the easier phonemic awareness skills to the more difficult. The following list is from easiest to more difficult.

> **Beginning and ending sounds**
>
> **Matching beginning and ending sounds**—fish/fight or run/fan
>
> **Isolating sounds**—identifying the first sound in the word
>
> **Substituting sounds**—change bl in black to tr
>
> **Blending sounds**—put these together: j-u-m-p
>
> **Segmenting sounds**—tell the sounds you hear in dog
>
> **Deleting sounds**—napkin without nap

TIP: While it is important to teach phonemic awareness, it is also critical to realize that some students master phonemic awareness while learning to read or after learning to read.

2. Students may benefit from having phonemic awareness linked to phonics instruction where the visual shapes of the letters are included.

Innovations

1. Using students' names for phonemic awareness activities is particularly effective.
2. Rhymes and rhyming books work particularly well for ending sounds. Students can brainstorm words that will work and then select their favorite words.

> EXAMPLE: Miss Muffet sat on a tuffet can be changed to Miss Hall sat on a wall.

3. Tongue twisters are effective for alliteration or beginning sounds.

> TIP: Use books such as *The Biggest Tongue Twister Book in the World* (1992) by Brandreth and Chin, *Z is for Zamboni* (2002) by Napier and Rose or *A My Name is Alice* (1992) by Bayer and Kellogg as examples of alliteration. Then students can create their own tongue twisters.

4. Alphabet books are wonderful for initial sounds and vocabulary building.

> TIP: Students can make their own alphabet sentences using students' names such as "Christian caught colorful caterpillars" or "Ethan eats enormous eggs."

Phonics

Definition: Phonics is understanding the relationship between letters and sounds in written text.

Why teach phonics?

Phonics is one of the tools students use when reading. Decoding helps students "sound out" unknown words.

What should phonics instruction look like?

1. Students are taught the alphabetic code where they learn to associate the sound with the letter—approximately 3 letters per week, preferably using meaningful words, students' names, or words from shared reading.

2. Once the letter sounds are learned, students move to onsets and rimes which are more effective for learning word patterns. The onsets are the letters before the vowel and the rimes begin with the vowel. 37 rimes allow students to read 500 primary words.

The 37 most common rimes are as follows:

-ack	-eat	-ice	-ock	-uck
-ail	-ell	-ick	-oke	-ug
-ain	-est	-ide	-op	-ump
-ake		-ight	-ore	-unk
-ale		-ill	-or	
-ame		-in		
-an		-ine		
-ank		-ing		
-ap		-ink		
-ash		-ip		
-at		-ir		
-ate				
-aw				
-ay				

Source: Marilyn J. Adams, 1990. *Beginning to Read: Thinking and Learning About Print*. Cambridge: MIT Press, pp. 321-322.

3. Phonics can be taught in many different ways, but the important considerations are that meaningful text is used for the instruction and that students are able to transfer their phonics skills to "real" reading.

4. Instruction is short—10-15 minutes per day of direct instruction and then reinforced throughout the day during reading and writing activities.

5. Phonics instruction can be whole group or part of the guided reading lesson. But, it must be interactive, engaging, and meet students' needs.

6. Phonics instruction should move from one-syllable words to multi-syllabic words using the rimes in each syllable to break words into parts.

What does phonics instruction NOT look like?

1. Instruction is rigid rather than based on students' needs.
2. The focus is on "the letter of the week."
3. Instruction utilizes isolated drill or worksheets.
4. All students are receiving the same instruction regardless of knowledge and need.

What materials should be used?

1. Reading materials that include decodable and high frequency words. The decodable words can be used for phonics instruction.
2. Stories that make sense.
3. Language that sounds like "real" language.
4. A large variety of phonics games, activities, manipulatives, and materials that can be used to reinforce instruction of meaningful text.

What do we know about phonics instruction?

1. Phonics instruction is important, but it is one, and only one, tool that students will use in reading.
2. By the time that students are reading at a fluent first-grade reading level, they are using patterns and analogies (onsets and rimes) rather than letter-by-letter decoding as their major decoding strategy.
3. The use of patterns and analogies will transfer to multi-syllabic or big words; however, this transfer will happen more quickly if specifically taught.
4. There is no research to support the use of only decodable materials.

Phonics Innovations

1. Children's names are an effective starting place for initial sounds.

   TIP: A name wall can be used to focus students on the initial sounds found in their names. This is where students' names are placed on cards and listed under the appropriate letter of the alphabet. Students can locate each other's names or use the name wall to write names (Wagstaff, 1999).

2. Making words is one way of teaching students to build words using letter sounds and patterns. The teacher provides students with letter cards or magnetic letters and then structures the lesson so students are practicing making particular words. The teacher usually limits the number of letters a student has at any one time.

   EXAMPLE: The teacher gives students six letters (a, c, e, g, r, t). The teacher may ask students to make the word *cat*. Then the teacher has students change one letter to make rat, add one letter to make rate, and change one letter to make gate. These lessons can be customized to meet students' needs (Cunningham, 1997).

3. Word walls can use the high-utility rimes to help focus students on patterns and analogies. This is where specific words are selected, written on cards, and then placed on the wall under the appropriate vowel.

    TIP: If *sack* is on the word wall, then *tack, rack,* and *black* are not put on the word wall. Only one word is added for each rime. Students then must generalize and find the pattern that helps them solve the new word. This strengthens decoding as well as spelling. Onsets and rimes can also be used for multi-syllabic words— students break the words into syllables and then find the pattern for each syllable.

    RESOURCE: Wagstaff's *Teaching Reading and Writing With Word Walls: Easy Lessons and Fresh Ideas for Creating Interactive Word Walls That Build Literacy Skills* (1999).

4. Modeled writing and interactive writing are ways of reinforcing phonics instruction.

    TIP: If students have just added -ide to the word wall, then other -ide words can be used in modeled or interactive writing instruction.

5. Phonics instruction must be balanced with high-frequency word instruction.

6. Only high-utility phonics rules should be taught.

    EXAMPLE: A rule such as when two vowels go walking, the first one does the talking applies only 45% of the time and therefore is not a high-utility rule. Also, rules are most effective if students generate the rule from words rather than being taught the rule.

    RESOURCE: Theodore Clymer's "The Utility of Phonic Generalizations in the Primary Grades." *Reading Teacher 50*(3), 182-187.

Non-Decodable, High-Frequency Words

Definition: Non-decodable, high-frequency words are words necessary for reading and writing that do not follow phonics rules.

Why teach non-decodable words?

These words are essential for developing automaticity and fluency.

What does non-decodable word instruction look like?

1. The focus is on the most frequently needed words in reading and writing.

2. Generally 3-5 words will be introduced each week.

3. Students will practice words in a variety of ways.

4. Students will be held accountable for the words that have been introduced.

5. Words selected for instruction will come from the texts being read.

What does non-decodable word instruction NOT look like?

1. Too many words are introduced.
2. Words are practiced only in isolation.

What materials should be used?

1. Instructional-level reading texts.
2. Word lists of high-frequency words.
3. Word walls or wall lists of high-frequency words.
4. Games, manipulatives, and other activities focusing on high-frequency, non-decodable words.

What do we know about high-frequency, non-decodable word instruction?

1. Instruction is essential for reading and writing success.
2. Words should be selected from reading materials or from students' writing samples.

> TIP: Students do better if taught two or three words at a time from the context of their reading materials. Once those words are mastered, other words can be added to the list.

> TIP: Teachers can identify the high-frequency words that appear in the books they will be using and then teach these words in context.

First-Grade High-Frequency Words

These words were taught over the course of one year.

about	only
again	our
are	people
any	put
because	said
been	some
before	the
boy	their
by	there
come	they
could	to
do	too
does	two
down	through
friend	use
from	very
girl	want
give	was
good	were
have	what
here	when
how	where
know	which
little	with
many	who
much	would
new	you
of	your
one	

Innovations for Teaching High-Frequency Words

1. Games such as Cunningham and Hall's "Be a Mind Reader" and "Guess the Covered Word" can be used to teach recognition of the high-frequency words.

   EXAMPLE: With "Be a Mind Reader," the teacher tells students he/she is thinking of a word that begins with a particular letter sound. Students predict a word. The teacher adds a new clue. Students then see if their predictions are still good or if they need to revise their predictions.

   EXAMPLE: "Guess the Covered" works much the same way, except the teacher uncovers the first letter, has students guess, then uncovers another letter, and so on until the word has been identified. (Cunningham & Hall, 1998)

2. The cloze procedure can be used for predicting high-frequency words. This is a strategy where a word is covered up and students try to predict the missing word using the context clues.

   TIP: A word is covered up with a sticky note. Students can brainstorm all the possibilities. Then one letter at a time can be uncovered with students changing their predictions as necessary.

3. Modeled writing and interactive writing can focus on the high-frequency words that students need to practice.

4. Multi-sensory activities improve both the reading and writing of non-decodable words.

   TIP: Students can stamp the words, trace the words, or use manipulatives to spell non-decodable, high-frequency words. One particularly effective strategy is to have students trace the words with their fingers after they have written the word in crayon.

Vocabulary Development

Definition: Learning the words that are critical to understanding the text.

Why is vocabulary instruction essential?

There is a direct correlation between vocabulary and comprehension. Rich and varied reading with a focus on vocabulary is the best way to enhance students' vocabulary development. We know that vocabulary deficiency is one of the primary causes of academic failure of disadvantaged students.

What should vocabulary instruction look like?

1. Students are actively engaged in learning new words.

   TIP: Words are more easily learned if students are constructing the meaning of the words, intrigued by the words, or can connect the words to their own lives.

2. Students' prior knowledge of essential story vocabulary should be informally assessed by the teacher. Words may be pre-taught if they are critical to understanding the text. If students have enough prior knowledge, they can determine the meaning from reading the text, and follow-up activities can focus on the new words.

   TIP: There are several questions the teacher can pose prior to having students read. Which words are most important? What do students know about the words?

3. New words are studied as connected concepts rather than isolated words.

   TIP: Semantic maps or graphic organizers can be used to show how the new word relates to known words.

4. There are multiple exposures to new words.

   TIP: Students can listen for the new word, watch for it in reading both at home and at school, have others use the new word, create a game using new words, or write a story incorporating the new words. Teachers can use new words throughout classroom instruction so that students can hear the word many times.

What should vocabulary instruction NOT look like?

1. Vocabulary study is not a list of words to be learned.

2. Activities are not dictionary definitions or writing a sentence using the word.

   RATIONALE: Too often students are unable to understand the dictionary definition or which dictionary definition they should select. Other activities are far more effective for learning new words.

What materials should be used?

Vocabulary can be taught through any materials being used in the classroom, including content area materials.

What do we know about vocabulary instruction?

1. The more students read, the better their vocabulary.

2. Students' vocabulary development will be enhanced if attention is focused on the words to be learned.

3. Meaning-based strategies are most successful.

4. Vocabulary instruction is essential for second-language learners and low-language students.

   RATIONALE: An average elementary student learns approximately 3,000 words per year or 8 per day (Hart & Risley, 1995). If a student falls behind, it is difficult to catch up.

5. To remember new words, students need approximately 8 to 15 meaningful encounters with each new word.

   TIP: Students can look for the new words in the newspaper, listen for the new words on television, or teach others the new words. The more times the words are used in meaningful contexts, the more likely they will be remembered.

6. Vocabulary instruction should include essential content words, multiple-meaning words, synonyms, antonyms, homonyms, and idioms.

    RESOURCE: *Words, Words, Words: Teaching Vocabulary in Grades 4-12* (1999) by Allen.

Vocabulary Development Innovations

1. **Vocabulary Word Cards** can be developed by students.

    TIP: Students can divide 5 x 7 cards into 4 parts. In different sections they identify the context in which the word is used, provide an example of what it is and what it is not, draw an illustration, or provide other characteristics. Students can then teach others their new words through a game format.

2. **A Linear Array** is where students place related words on a continuum.

    EXAMPLE: Freezing…cool…tepid…hot…boiling

3. **Sticky Flag Notes** can be used to identify words in context that are new or used in a new way.

    TIP: When students are reading and come upon an unknown word, they can ask the following questions. Do I know the word in another context? Do I need to know the word? How can I figure out the word? Students can return to the sticky notes after completing the reading. This is less disruptive to comprehension and often students will be able to determine the meaning as they continue reading.

4. **Typographic Clues** is a strategy where students are taught to use text clues to figure out the words. These include bolding, italics, footnotes, pictures, charts, and graphs.

    TIP: This is particularly effective with science and social studies texts that use different text structures to identify new vocabulary words.

5. **Semantic Clues** teach students to use the context to solve the meaning. For example, students might look for synonyms or antonyms, definitions, examples, comparisons, and contrasts that are provided in the text.

    TIP: Content area materials are great sources for semantic clues. Science and social studies books will usually provide definitions for terms by providing a synonym or an example.

6. **Word Collections** encourage students to build lists or collections of words.

    EXAMPLES: Some categories could include: Loud words, wet words, grumpy words, odd words, convincing words, color words, or silly words.

7. **Word of the Week** has students select a high-utility word of the week. This word must be used a minimum of fifteen times during the week.

    TIP: Dramatizing words or using charades helps students learn the word of the week.

8. **Idioms** can be collected and then illustrated.

TIP: This is a great activity for English as a Second Language or English Language Learners.

RESOURCE: *Scholastic Dictionary of Idioms* (1998) by Terban.

9. **Alliterations** can be created using words that have been studied in different content areas.

EXAMPLE: A weather unit might lead to, "Windy weather wakes weathermen."

10. Students can **collect words that they like the sound of** such as abracadabra, gazebo, whoosh, astronaut, chrysanthemum, and so on.

11. Students can **collect words from their reading that meet a particular criterion**: describing words, character words, or action words.

TIP: These words can be posted in the classroom and referred to when students are writing.

12. Students can make **word lists for overused words**.

TIP: Select words that are overused in students' writing and have them generate other options for words such as "nice, good, said, or run."

13. **Grammar skills** can be addressed as a part of vocabulary development.

TIP: Students can select a passage and replace all adjectives or all verbs with more interesting words.

14. **Illustrations** can help students remember new words.

TIP: This is particularly true for low-language students or English as a Second Language students.

ELEMENT 2

LANGUAGE STRUCTURE

Definition: Understanding how written language works. Also, called syntax.

Why teach language structure?

It is one more tool essential for reading comprehension and successful writing. Instruction in language structure is critical for second-language learners and low-language students.

What does language structure instruction look like?

1. It is most effective when examples are selected from reading or writing materials.

2. Mini-lessons are an effective way of providing instruction that positively impacts both reading and writing.

3. Instruction is purposeful and based on students' identified needs. Students' needs are determined by observing students' during reading and writing.

RESOURCE: *Teaching Grammar in Context* (1996) by Weaver.

What does language structure instruction NOT look like?

1. Grammar books with isolated skill instruction.

2. Asking low-language or second-language learners "if it sounds right?"

    RATIONALE: They will always say, "Yes," and then the teacher is left explaining why it is wrong. It is better to repeat it correctly, either with or without an explanation.

What materials should be used?

1. Reading materials

2. Read alouds

3. Students' writing samples

What do we know about language structure instruction?

1. Syntax presents unique challenges for low-language or second-language learners.

2. The best way to teach students the syntactical cuing system is to provide multiple opportunities for reading and hearing language.

3. Having students use the instructed language structures in their writing will reinforce the skills taught during reading.

    TIP: If instruction focuses on complex sentences, then students should be expected to use complex sentences appropriately in their writing.

Language Structure Innovations

1. **Lift the Sentence** is a strategy that focuses on removing one sentence from a literary resource and then having the teacher and students discuss the syntax of the sentence.

2. **Syntax Search** is a strategy where students look through different materials to find examples of the skill being taught. These can be put on posters or in notebooks for future reference.

    EXAMPLE: Students might look for dialogue, commas in a series, or sentences beginning with a phrase.

3. **Ruth Heller's books** can be used to teach parts of speech.

    TIP: *Many Luscious Lollipops: A Book About Adjectives* (1989) can be used for language structure, parts of speech, and vocabulary development. The phrase, "A WET and SOGGY, DRIZZLY day, RAINY, WINTERY and GRAY," lends itself to much discussion. This is a great activity for high-achieving students.

4. **Expanded Sentences** is a strategy where students look at sentences to see how the author has expanded the sentence by adding phrases, adjectives, and so on to the basic sentence.

    TIP: Students can take a complex sentence and determine the basic or core sentence.

5. **Sentence Combining** is a method for teaching students how writers combine sentences by using conjunctions, phrases, etc.

> TIP: Students can take complex sentences and break them into their parts or reverse the process by combining short sentences.

> RESOURCES: William Strong's *Sentence Combining: A Composing Book* (1994) and *Writer's Toolbox: A Sentence Combining Workshop* (1995).

6. **Verb Forms** has students look for all the different forms of a particular verb so that students can see the many different ways a verb can be used.

> TIP: This is particularly effective with irregular verbs.

7. **Modeled Writing** can be used to model the language structures being taught.

ELEMENT 3

FLUENCY

Definition: Fluency is multidimensional and includes reading at an appropriate rate with a high degree of smoothness and accuracy with appropriate phrasing, intonation, and expressiveness.

Why teach fluency?

Fluency can impact comprehension.

What does fluency instruction look like?

1. Teachers model fluent reading through read alouds, shared reading, and read alongs.

> TIP: The teacher can point out fluency strategies including phrasing, rate of reading, and expressiveness. Hearing fluent reading helps students improve their fluency.

2. Teachers encourage students to do repeated readings.

> TIP: Students can do repeated readings by reading to a younger student, tape recording a text, reading to a volunteer, rereading at home, or reading as a readers theater. It is important that the repeated readings be motivational.

3. Students are practicing in independent-level materials.

> RATIONALE: To establish fluency, students need to be reading materials that are at their independent level—95% word recognition with comprehension.

4. Students have an opportunity to read silently prior to reading aloud.

> TIP: If students read the text silently prior to being asked to read aloud, they will improve their fluency. To judge students' fluency, they should have had an opportunity to read silently prior to reading aloud.

5. Teachers focus students' attention on phrases rather than single words.

> TIP: Students who read word by word will lose fluency. By underlining the phrases

or putting phrases on sentence strips, the teacher can focus on phrases rather than single words.

6. Students have numerous opportunities for developing self-monitoring.

> RATIONALE: Some students lose fluency because they are waiting for the teacher to correct their reading. If students learn to self-correct, they will improve their fluency.

What does fluency instruction NOT look like?

1. Fluency instruction is NOT just rate of reading.

2. Fluency instruction is NOT just repeated readings.

What materials should be used?

Any independent-level materials may be used.

What do we know about fluency instruction?

1. Students will become more fluent readers with instruction.

2. Rate of reading is one component, but only one component, of fluency instruction.

> TIP: Students at Grade 1 should read approximately 60 wpm, Grade 2 70 wpm, and Grade 3 75-85 wpm.

3. Comprehension is impacted by fluency.

Fluency Innovations

1. **Taped readings** can be used to improve students' fluency. Students can listen to fluent tapes made by students, cross-age tutors, parents, or volunteers.

2. **Meaningful phrases** can be identified by using highlighter tape or highlighter pens. Also, phrases can be underlined on overhead transparencies or written on pocket chart cards.

3. **Readers' theater** or reading performances can be used to increase fluency and expression.

> TIP: Students can write their own readers' theater, adapting favorite books such as Pat Hutchins' *The Doorbell Rang* (1986) or Patricia Polacco's *Pink and Say* (1994).

4. **Poetry, jump rope jingles, and chants** can be read aloud, focusing on the rhythm of the language.

5. At the intermediate level, **teachers may read the first paragraph** or approximately 100 words to model the author's language prior to having students read the text.

6. **Choral reading** can encourage fluency.

> TIP: A choral reading piece can be placed on the overhead, divided into parts, and then practiced. Songs can be written out and used as choral reading pieces.

7. **Echo reading** promotes fluency. The teacher can read a portion of a text and students can echo what the teacher has just read. This can be done with shared reading materials.

ELEMENT 4

COMPREHENSION

Definition: Understanding what was read—the purpose of reading.

Why teach comprehension?

All students will perform at higher levels in both reading and writing if comprehension skills are taught. Comprehension will be strengthened if three conditions are met: IF students are engaged in the reading; IF students are taught specific reading comprehension strategies; and IF these strategies transfer to their independent reading. In many programs, comprehension is assessed but not taught. If we want students to comprehend better, then comprehension must be specifically taught.

What does comprehension instruction look like?

1. Pre-reading, during-reading, and after-reading strategies are modeled and taught.
2. Comprehension strategies are applied in a wide variety of materials.
3. Students are engaged, interested, and successful.
4. Strategies should aid comprehension, but the instruction should not take more time than the reading.

What does comprehension instruction NOT look like?

1. Comprehension is assessed with little or no instruction.
2. Focus is on follow-up questions.
3. Students are going through the motions of reading, but do not understand what they are reading.
4. Students are uninterested in what is being read and are not relating the material to their own lives.

What do we know about comprehension instruction?

1. Pre-reading strategies can assess prior knowledge, build background knowledge, introduce essential vocabulary, encourage prediction, and/or engage students in the upcoming material.
2. During-reading strategies can keep students focused on what they are reading, keep them engaged, and hold them accountable for what they are reading.

3. After-reading strategies enhance and extend comprehension by helping students link the reading to their own lives, by encouraging higher-level thinking, by clarifying misconceptions, and by making the text more relevant.

4. Specific strategy instruction will strengthen students' understanding of different genres and formats.

5. Comprehension strategy instruction is most effective when aligned to students' needs.

Comprehension Innovations

1. The same comprehension strategies can be taught across the grades by using different levels of sophistication or different materials. This can build a sense of community within the school and strengthen students' reading.

2. Strategies can be introduced and modeled with the whole class, but these strategies are most effective if taught and applied during guided reading instruction.

3. Graphic organizers or visual ways of presenting information are often outstanding ways of helping students enhance their comprehension.

    RESOURCES: *Graphic Organizers to Use With Any Book* (1999) by O'Brien-Palmer and *Teaching Reading in the Content Areas: If Not Me, Then Who?* (1998) by Billmeyer and Barton.

4. Strategies can be posted in the classroom, and students can be asked to identify the strategies they are using during literature circles or independent reading. This will help students transfer these strategies to their independent reading. The following pages show several specific examples of comprehension strategies.

SPECIFIC EXAMPLES OF COMPREHENSION STRATEGIES

Pre-Reading Strategies

Anticipation Guides

A. The teacher creates a series of meaningful questions based on the material to be read (Herber, 1978).

B. Prior to reading, each student agrees or disagrees with each statement. This is followed by a short discussion.

C. As students read the text they watch for information, change their predictions if necessary, and note the page where the information was found.

D. Following the reading, students discuss what they have learned, what surprised them, and what new questions they might have. This strategy is particularly effective with content area material.

EXAMPLE 1: Primary—*Miss Rumphius* (1982) by Barbara Cooney.

Answer yes or no and support your response.

	You	The Author
1. Living alone all your life would be lonely.		
2. People are responsible for making the world a more beautiful place.		
3. Goals can be accomplished.		
4. Traveling to faraway places can be dangerous.		
5. Each person can change nature.		

EXAMPLE 2: Intermediate—*A Whaling Community of the 1840s* (2002) by Gare Thompson.

Answer T or F in the left column prior to reading.
Use the right column to verify your prediction or change your response.

Before Reading			During Reading		
T	F	1. Twelve-year-olds can sail on whaling ships.	T	F	p#____
T	F	2. If your house is near the water, it means you are rich.	T	F	p#____
T	F	3. In 1840 everyone's jobs in New Bedford centered on whaling.	T	F	p#____
T	F	4. The crew help write the rules of the ship.	T	F	p#____
T	F	5. Cooks on whalers prepare healthy, tasty meals.	T	F	p#____
T	F	6. The whalers tow the whales to shore.	T	F	p#____
T	F	7. All parts of the whale are used.	T	F	p#____
T	F	8. Whaling ended because whales became endangered animals.	T	F	p#____

Predicting From Clues

There are several options with this strategy.

A. The teacher may use three to four photos from the book, not necessarily shown to the students in sequence. After each photo or illustration students predict what the story/text will be about.

B. Another way of doing this strategy is to collect three to five objects from the story; the teacher shows all of the objects; and students again predict what the story might be about.

C. A third way is to provide students with five to six words or phrases taken from the text, and these are used to predict the story. As students read the story, they watch for each object, word, or phrase to appear. They can put sticky notes in the appropriate places.

The follow-up is to have students compare their predictions to the author's story or text. Often students will choose to write their own stories because they like their versions better than the one written by the author.

EXAMPLE 1: Primary Using Objects—*Miss Rumphius* (1982) by Barbara Cooney.

> Students are shown the following objects: a seed packet of lupines, a miniature camel, a kangaroo, a coconut, and a mother of pearl shell. Students predict a story that includes all of the objects.

EXAMPLE 2: Intermediate Using Pictures—*Nettie's Trip South* (1987) by Ann Turner.

> Students are shown 4 pictures from the book and asked to predict what it will be about.

EXAMPLE 3: Upper Primary Using Words/Phrases—*Moss Gown* (1987) by William H. Hooks.

> Students are shown the following 5 phrases and asked to predict the story:
> A skittering wind splashed rain against the tall columns
> How sad and discouraged he looked
> The slender black gris-gris woman
> The murky, gray-green swamp
> They snickered behind his back

Building From Vocabulary

The teacher selects approximately 10 to 15 words from the text, and prior to reading students will use these words. Here are several different optional activities that can be selected by the teacher. These activities can be done individually or with partners. Teachers can monitor and decide if any other type of vocabulary introduction is needed prior to reading.

A. Students might sort the words into categories and then predict the story.

B. They might create a semantic web to show how the words are related to one another.

C. Students can also sort the words into those known and those unknown.

D. Students then read the text and look for the vocabulary words. They can label an identified word with a sticky note or record the page number on their word card.

E. As a follow-up they can compare their initial projections to the actual word usage.

F. Students may write a paragraph connecting these words.

G. They can illustrate some of the words.

H. They can teach some of the words to another student.

EXAMPLE 1: Primary—*Miss Rumphius* (1982) by Barbara Cooney.

jungle	grandfather	wharves	artist	faraway
tropical	surrounded	scattered	lupines	camel
sailing	sparkled	patches	conservatory	bird of paradise

EXAMPLE 2: Intermediate—*My Prairie Year* (1986) by Brett Harvey.

| anchored | plastered | canvas | boardwalk | silent |
| crouched | feverishly | transfixed | proprietor | intense |

Character Clues

Strategy Steps

A. Teachers can choose words that describe one or two characters from the text.

B. If using words to describe only one character, students talk about what kind of person they expect to find in the story. If using words describing two characters, students sort the words into two columns (one for each character) and discuss the characters.

C. As students read, they look for information that matches the characteristics.

D. At the completion of the reading, students write a character description for one character.

E. Also, students can participate in an after-reading strategy by comparing themselves to one of the characters.

EXAMPLE 1: Primary With One Character—*Miss Rumphius* (1982) by Barbara Cooney.

adventurous	artist	family member
senior citizen	responsible	friendly
determined	accepting	storyteller

EXAMPLE 2: Intermediate With Two Characters—*The Whipping Boy* (1986) by Sid Fleischman.

Sort the words into two categories and describe the two characters, Jemmy and Horace.

mistreated	victim	generous	rude
orphan	problem solver	gloating	hurtful
stubborn	teasing	clever	educated
kind	selfish	smirking	bored

Cloze Sentences

Strategy Steps

A. The teacher selects four to five sentences with critical vocabulary from the text.

B. The sentences are presented to the students with missing words.

C. Individually, in partners, or as a group, students brainstorm words that would fit in the sentences.

D. As students read, they hunt for the sentences and compare their word choices to that of the author.

EXAMPLE 1: Primary With One Character—*Miss Rumphius* (1982) by Barbara Cooney.

> From the front stoop she could see the wharves and the _____ masts of the tall ships.
>
> In the evening Alice sat on her grandfather's knee and listened to his stories of _____ places.
>
> Miss Rumphius went to a real _____ island, where people kept cockatoos and monkeys as pets.
>
> Miss Rumphius watched the sun come up; she watched it cross the heavens and _____ on the water.

EXAMPLE 2: Intermediate—*Saturn* (1985) by Seymour Simon.

> These stars were called planets, from a Greek word that means _____.
>
> Saturn is mostly made up of _____.
>
> He was _____ to see what looked like ears on either side of the planet.
>
> _____ is an invisible force that makes raindrops and snow crystals fall to the ground.
>
> Saturn is the _____ object in the night sky.

During-Reading Strategies

These strategies are based on the pre-reading strategies explained earlier.

Anticipation Guide Follow-Up	Students keep the anticipation guide out during their reading. As they find information that confirms or rejects their hypotheses, they note the correct answer and the page number where they found the information.
Revising the Predictions	Students read the material keeping in mind their Predicting From Clues predictions. Students make two lists—information that supports their predictions and information that causes them to revise their predictions.
Finding Vocabulary	Students watch for the vocabulary that was introduced in Building From Vocabulary. As they locate the words, they place a sticky flag next to the word. At the end of the reading, they discuss the words and how they were used. This can be done in partners or as a part of a guided reading follow-up.
Character Proof	Students use their predictions from Character Clues. As they read they look for descriptions that support their predictions or that force them to revise their predictions.
Author's Choice	Students locate the Cloze Sentences. They compare their predictions to the author's word choices. After completing the reading, students discuss the word choices.

Copy Search

Strategy Steps

A. Students look for particular items in the text. For example, if they are studying great openers in writing, they could look for ways the writer opens the entire book, chapters, or sections of the book. If they are studying transitions, they could look for transition words used by the author.

B. These are identified with sticky notes.

C. Following the reading, one or two favorites are copied down. The ones copied down can go on a wall poster or in a notebook.

D. Students can refer back to these when doing their own writing.

Example 1: Primary, Descriptive Words—*The Rag Coat* (1991) by Lauren Mills.

Dirty fingers

Yellow-golds of the birch leaves

The silvery grays and purples of the sky

Porcelain doll

A faded piece from a fancy dress

Example 2: Intermediate, Openers—*The Crossing* (1987) by Gary Paulsen.

"Manny Bustos awakened when the sun cooked the cardboard over his head and heated the box he was sleeping in until even a lizard could not have taken it, and he knew, suddenly, that it was time."

"In the usual flow of his life things had to work very fast for Manny or not at all. Manny sat in the dark and waited."

Graphic Organizers

As students read they can complete a graphic organizer that helps them identify the key parts of the text being read. Graphic organizers can be used for many skills, including:

- story sequence
- story mapping
- timelines
- cause and effect
- main idea and details

They are one way of providing a visual representation of the information while holding students accountable for the reading.

Example 1: Primary—Sequence—*If You Give a Mouse a Cookie* (1985) by Laura Joffe.

Students can identify the sequence of the book. This can lead to writing their own books.

If you give a mouse a cookie, he is going to want a _____.

If you give a mouse a _____, he is going to want a _____.

And so on....

Example 2: Intermediate—Main Ideas and Details—*Saturn* (1985) by Seymour Simon.

Students are asked to find out three details for each of the three categories.

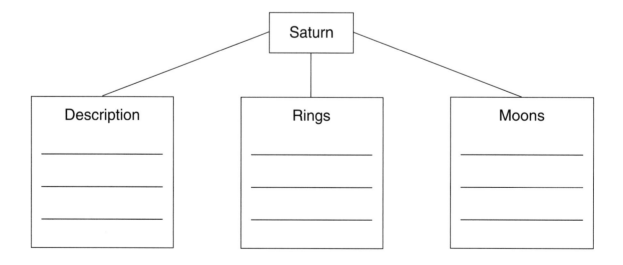

After-Reading Strategies

So What Does This Have to Do With Me?

Following the reading of a text, the teacher engages students in an activity where students identify how the text had a personal impact on them. This strategy works well with both fiction and nonfiction material. Graphic organizers such as Venn diagrams or T-charts can be used.

Example 1: Primary—*The Rag Coat* (1991) by Lauren Mills.

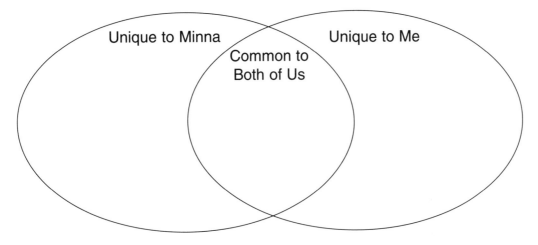

Example 2: Intermediate—*The Earth is My Mother* (2000) by Bev Doolittle.

Students can relate the issues to their own lives.

What does protecting our environment have to do with me?

Fact or Fiction?

Strategy Steps

A. Students read two paired books or pieces of text, one fiction and one nonfiction.*

B. They then create two columns of information—one for facts and one for fictional information.

C. The follow-up discussion can focus on whether fiction writers include facts and whether nonfiction writers include nonfactual information.

Example 1: Primary

	Fictional Info	Factual Info
Owls (Newbridge)	_____ _____ _____	_____ _____ _____
Owl Babies (2002) by Waddell	_____ _____ _____	_____ _____ _____

Example 2: Intermediate

	Fictional Info	Factual Info
Tornadoes (2001) Simon	_____ _____ _____	_____ _____ _____
Night of the Twister (1986) by Ruckman or *The Case of the Swirling Killer Tornado* (1998) by Erickson	_____ _____	_____ _____

*The same strategy can be done with fact/opinion by pairing a factual article with an editorial or opinion article.

Questioning the Text

Strategy Steps

A. During reading students place sticky notes on things they think they might want to question.

B. Then after reading the text, students generate questions. These questions can be ones they would like to ask the author about the content, style, or format. Students can be encouraged to ask higher-level questions.

C. The questions can be discussed with classmates or additional information can be obtained by contacting the author with their questions, sending their questions to an expert in the field via email, or researching the topic further.

Example 1: Primary—Questioning the Author—*With Love, Little Red Hen* (2001) by Ada

> Format Questions:
>> Why did you choose to write the book as a collection of letters?
>> How did you sequence the letters?

Example 2: Primary—Content Questions—*Ice Mummy: The Discovery of a 5,000 Year-Old-Man* (1998).

> How can they tell how old the mummy is?
> How do they know he is from Italy?
> Why would he have such light clothing in such cold weather?
> What would his home have been like?
> What else do we know about life in that area 5,000 years ago?

Example 3: Intermediate—Questioning the Author and Content—*A Whaling Community of the 1840s* (2002) by Thompson.

> Format Questions:
>> How did you decide which chapters to include?
>> Did you have other information that you left out?
>> Where did you find your information?
>
> Content Questions:
>> What other industries supported the whalers?
>> How large is a whaling boat?
>> How do the sailors get fresh food?
>> Why would people want to work on a whaler?
>> Why are whales protected today?

Writing From a Unique Point of View

After reading a selection, students write an article about what they've read from a particular point of view. For example, if the article is about forest fires, they might write from the point of view of one of the animals, a naturalist, a home owner, or a forest ranger. This helps students see that often the way in which an event is described is impacted by the role of the viewer.

Example 1: Primary—*The True Story of the Three Little Pigs by A. Wolf* (1995) by Scieszka.

> After hearing the book written from the wolf's point of view, students can then take another tale and write it from a different point of view such as Cinderella from the stepsisters' point of view or Goldilocks from the bears' point of view.

Example 2: Intermediate—*After the Spill: The Exxon Valdez Disaster, Then and Now* (1999) by Markle.

> Students can read and research the oil spill and then write from different points of view—the insurance company, the environmentalist, the ship's captain, or one of the birds.
>
> *Newspaper articles often lend themselves to this strategy.

Summary

It is critical that all of the elements of reading instruction be a part of the reading program. Word study helps students decode and understand the meanings of the words. Instruction in language structure enhances comprehension and strengthens writing by focusing on the unique features of written language. Comprehension is the goal. Pre-reading strategies engage students in the material, provide the necessary background knowledge, and introduce critical vocabulary. During-reading strategies keep students focused on what they are reading and hold them accountable for the reading. After-reading strategies extend students' thinking and help students connect the reading to their own lives. Each is a critical part of reading instruction.

Checklist for Elements of Reading Instruction

Rate each item on a 1-4 scale.

	Low			High
1. All four elements (word study, structure of language, fluency, and comprehension) are included.	1	2	3	4
2. Phonemic awareness and phonics lessons are short (10-15 minutes each day).	1	2	3	4
3. Students not needing phonics instruction are doing other activities.	1	2	3	4
4. Onsets and rimes are taught when students have mastered letter sounds.	1	2	3	4
5. Onsets and rimes are taught by analogy, using something like a word wall.	1	2	3	4
6. Non-decodable words are part of the instructional program.	1	2	3	4
7. Essential vocabulary is effectively taught.	1	2	3	4
8. Vocabulary instruction is engaging, active, and builds connections for students.	1	2	3	4
9. Language structure is a focus of reading instruction.	1	2	3	4
10. Fluency instruction is a part of the reading program.	1	2	3	4
11. Comprehension is taught (not just assessed).	1	2	3	4
12. Pre-reading strategies are consistently used.	1	2	3	4
13. During-reading strategies are used to keep students focused on what they are reading.	1	2	3	4
14. After-reading strategies are used to help students connect to the text, clarify misunderstandings, or extend the text.	1	2	3	4

SCORING: Any area scoring below a 3 needs further review.

Copyright © 2004 by Corwin Press. All rights reserved. Reprinted from *The Book of Reading and Writing Ideas, Tips, and Lists for the Elementary Classroom* by Sandra E. Anderson. Thousand Oaks, CA: Corwin Press, www.corwinpress.com. Reproduction authorized only for the local school site that has purchased this book.

Chapter 4
Components of an Effective, Complete Writing Program

> **Success Story**
>
> *Elementary students were not doing well on persuasive writing, which was one measure of writing performance. When students read persuasive pieces, identified the characteristics of persuasive writing, and then wrote their own persuasive pieces, writing scores soared. The key seemed to be starting with reading and having students construct the characteristics of persuasive writing.*

There are five components of an effective, complete writing program. Each of these is critical to strengthening students' writing.

Modeled writing provides an opportunity for teachers to select specific skills, tailor the instruction to meet students' needs, and model the writing process. Modeled writing is more frequently used at the primary grades, but can also effectively be used with intermediate students.

Interactive writing is "sharing" the pen with students as they are able to successfully contribute to the writing. It is generally done on large chart paper with the whole class or a small group.

Structured writing is teaching students how to do specific types of writing. This component is critical because it can align to state standards and assessments.

Writers workshop lets the student select the format and topic of the writing. Its strength is the fact that students have choice.

Independent writing provides time for students to write.

Using each of these components strengthens students' writing.

COMPONENT 1

MODELED WRITING

Definition: The teacher models the writing process on chart paper or an overhead projector using a think-aloud process to describe the writing process to students.

Why use modeled writing?

Modeled writing provides an opportunity for the teacher to model concepts of print and writing techniques that align to the skills needed by students.

What does modeled writing look like?

1. The teacher composes the text. Students may be observers or may make suggestions.

2. The teacher reinforces previously taught skills and intentionally selects one or two new skills or formats to teach based on students' needs.

3. Students' needs are identified by observing their writing.

4. Modeled writing can be done with the whole group or small groups.

5. With emergent and early readers, illustrations may be used to support the text.

6. With fluent readers, modeled writing can be used when introducing new formats or new skills.

7. Modeled writing should occur daily with emergent and early readers.

8. Sessions are short—approximately 10-15 minutes.

9. Students have opportunities to do their own writing following the modeled writing lessons.

> RESOURCE: *Using Modeled Writing to Maximize Your Students' Growth in Writing and Reading, K-1*, Bureau of Education & Research Video.

What does modeled writing NOT look like?

1. Teachers completing the writing before students are present.

2. Teachers using a specific sequence of skills without taking into consideration students' needs.

Suggested Skill List for Modeled or Interactive Writing:

1. **Concepts of Print**
   top to bottom
   left to right
   return sweep
   2-finger spaces
   1-to-1 correspondence

2. **Word Study**
   initial & ending sounds, onsets and rimes
   high frequency words
   word choice
   parts of speech

3. **Language Structure and Conventions**
   capitalization
   periods
   question marks
   exclamation marks
   commas
   apostrophes
   quotation marks
   verb tense
   complete sentences
   pronouns
   sentence expansion

4. **Content**
   beginning, middle, & end
   logical organization
   openers
   voice
   main idea and details
   illustrations to support text
   point of view
   genre
   format
   revision

What materials should be used?

1. Stories or text can be based on events in the teacher's life, students' lives, or responses to text.

2. Materials needed include chart paper with felt pens, or overhead transparencies with overhead pens.

3. Ed Emberley's drawing books may be used for samples of simple illustrations.

What do we know about modeled writing?

1. Many students learn to read from writing—approximately 20-33%.

2. Modeled writing increases students' success in both reading and writing.

3. Modeled writing provides teachers with multiple opportunities to teach specific skills.

Modeled Writing Innovations

1. Modeled writing charts can be posted as part of a print-rich environment and used for practice reading.

2. Modeled writing can be used for social studies, science, or math instruction.

    TIP: Modeled writing can be used for introducing new topics prior to studying a unit of study, or it can be used as a review strategy after studying a particular topic.

3. Modeled writing can focus on one theme over several days, such as writing about a field trip.

4. Modeled writing can include personal stories of students in the classroom, such as important events or happenings. Students enjoy writing and reading about each other.

COMPONENT 2

INTERACTIVE WRITING

Definition: Teacher and students compose text together with the teacher sharing the pen with students as they become more proficient writers.

Why use interactive writing?

Interactive writing provides instruction precisely at the point of students' needs. It moves students from seeing writing being done to being a part of the writing process. It provides opportunities for students to use what they know about writing including hearing sounds in words, concepts of print, and other writing skills.

What does interactive writing look like?

1. The text is composed by the teacher and students. Individual students share the pen with

the teacher—individuals are asked to come up and write a particular letter, show spacing, write a word, or participate in any other way that builds success.

2. It may be done in small groups or with the whole group.

3. Students sit around chart paper or the overhead projector and as appropriate the teacher hands the pen to the students.

4. Lessons are short in duration, but are strategically focused on students' writing needs based on the teacher's observations of students' writing.

5. The charts become part of the environmental print.

6. Word walls become part of the instruction as students refer to the classroom word walls when sharing the pen.

7. Students who are not using the pen are actively engaged in what is going on. For example, they may be writing the first letter of a word or an entire word on individual dry erasable boards or they may be telling a partner what should be written.

What does interactive writing NOT look like?

1. The teacher doing all the work.

2. Students not engaged in the writing process.

3. Topics being written about are of little interest to students.

What materials should be used?

1. Chart paper with felt pens or overhead transparencies with overhead pens.

2. Correction tape, or white tape, which can be put over any mistakes.

3. Individual dry erasable boards or chalk boards.

    TIP: Shower board may be purchased in sheets and cut into inexpensive individual dry erasable boards.

What do we know about interactive writing?

1. Students become more confident, competent writers when they participate in interactive writing.

2. Interactive writing charts are effective ways to provide reading practice materials.

3. Interactive writing is highly effective with emergent, early, and struggling writers.

4. Interactive writing is an outstanding way to teach specific reading and writing skills.

    TIP: Interactive writing is an ideal way to introduce and teach many different skills, including story retelling, sentence structure, word choice, and grammar/punctuation skills.

    RESOURCE: *Using INTERACTIVE WRITING to Strengthen Your Students' Phonemic Awareness and Phonics Skills, K-1*, Bureau of Education & Research Video.

Interactive Writing Innovations

1. Class newsletters can be created during the interactive writing session.

2. Using students' names in the writing is highly motivational.

3. A community of learners can be enhanced through interactive writing.

   EXAMPLE: Students in one class wrote to a secret classroom visitor. Students carried on a continuing dialogue with their secret visitor. The secret visitor left notes for the students. This promoted an interest in reading and writing. Students couldn't wait to see the new messages.

4. Messages can be written to staff members, the office staff, the principal, or other people.

5. The teacher can select skills that align to standardized testing and use interactive writing as one more way of reinforcing students' knowledge in areas that will be assessed.

6. Interactive writing can be used to reinforce content area learning. It is ideal for summarizing what has been learned.

COMPONENT 3

STRUCTURED WRITING

Definition: Teacher selects the writing topic, format or mode and provides instruction in the craft of writing. This may align to state writing assessments.

Why use structured writing?

Structured writing provides opportunities for teachers to introduce and teach many different modes of writing—pattern, narrative, descriptive, persuasive, explanatory, procedural, or expository. Structured writing can be used to teach the various skills of writing, including ideas and content, organization, creativity, voice, word choice, sentence structure, conventions, genre, and formats. Structured writing instruction is essential if students are to achieve success on writing assessments.

What does structured writing look like?

1. With emergent readers, the topics selected for structured writing will be less complex and aligned to students' reading levels.

   TIP: It may involve pattern writing using a familiar pattern taken from a literature book.

2. With more fluent readers and writers the teacher will design a lesson around a particular mode of writing aligned to standards. Reading and writing samples will be shared by the teacher. Students will determine the key characteristics of this type of writing. Students can collect other samples and compare the samples to the key characteristics. Students

can then write their own samples. These samples will be shared and evaluated.

> TIP: If a rubric or scoring form is developed, it can be used by students for self-assessment and by the teacher for evaluation. These rubrics can then be compared—usually students' self-evaluations are more critical than the teacher's evaluation.

3. Structured writing instruction can be done with whole groups or small groups.
4. Students receive specific feedback on their writing.

> TIP: Mechanics and content should be evaluated separately. When working with emergent writers, they will write more if the initial focus is on content.

What does structured writing NOT look like?

1. Students having total choice of topic and format. There will be limited choice, but students are expected to meet the criteria.
2. Students being assigned writing without seeing examples or without instruction.

What materials should be used?

Vast quantities of literature and content area materials should be used as examples.

What do we know about structured writing?

1. Students get better at writing by writing.
2. Students who read more, write better. Also, students who read more variety are able to write with greater variety.
3. To improve on writing assessments, students must be taught to write using the same criteria on which they will be evaluated.
4. It is important to expose students to a wide variety of writing styles and modes.
5. Students benefit from determining the key characteristics of different types of writing.
6. Students will be better writers if they develop the rubrics that will be used for evaluation and are involved in self-assessing their writing.
7. Specific feedback is essential for improvement.

Structured Writing Innovations

1. Students can create key descriptors for different modes of writing and post these in the room.

   > EXAMPLE: For descriptive writing, students came up with the following criteria.

   - The writer uses many details
   - The writer uses lots of adjectives
   - The writer makes the reader feels like he or she was there
   - The writing is well organized and easy to follow

2. Great Openers—students can create notebooks or wall charts of great openers.

   TIP: This same strategy can be used for other literary areas—character descriptions, settings, use of metaphors, and so on.

3. Software can be used for brainstorming, webbing, or creating flow charts. A web or flow chart can be a part of the writing process. One source is Inspiration Software (www.inspiration.com).

4. One particular topic can be used for all of the different modes.

   EXAMPLE: Students can select a favorite product, such as Oreos. They can then write descriptive, persuasive, explanatory, and narrative paragraphs about the product. This helps students understand the different modes of writing.

5. Students can create a description card for an object without naming the object. Other students can guess the object.

6. Students can explore titles used by other authors and discuss what makes a title interesting. This can also be done with newspaper headlines.

7. Students can write from different points of view or for different audiences to help understand how the writing might change.

   EXAMPLE: Students can read about logging. They can then write persuasive pieces from the point of view of a homeowner, a forest ranger, an animal living in the forest, an environmentalist, a logger, or a paper product company.

8. After a particular skill has been taught, students can apply the skill in their writing and, as a part of their revision, students can identify where they have applied the skill.

   EXAMPLE: After thesis sentences had been taught, students were expected to include a thesis sentence in their writing. Students identified and highlighted their thesis sentences.

9. Students can improve nonfiction writing by reading several nonfiction texts and discussing key characteristics.

   TIP: It is helpful to model with the whole group and to have small groups write a nonfiction piece prior to having individual students write their own.

   RESOURCE: *Is That a Fact? Teaching Nonfiction Writing K-3* (2002) by Stead.

10. Mini-lessons are effective ways of teaching specific skills.

   EXAMPLE: Writing an Eye-Catching Lead—Students can learn from examples how informational writers use fictional writing strategies to make their leads come alive.

   EXAMPLE: Airing the Opposing Point of View—Students can strengthen their persuasive writing by including the opposing view in their arguments. (Portalupi & Fletcher, 2001)

   RESOURCES: *Craft Lessons: Teaching Writing K-8* (1999) and *Nonfiction Craft Lessons: Teaching Information Writing K-8* (2001) by Portalupi and Fletcher.

COMPONENT 4

WRITERS WORKSHOP

Why use writers workshop?

Students are often more motivated when they choose their writing topics and formats.

What does writers workshop look like?

1. Teachers present mini-lessons to the whole class, small groups, or individuals.
2. Mini-lessons are focused on students' needs and determined by reviewing students' writings.
3. Teachers record the status of the class or what each individual will be working on that day.
4. Students are on-task and spend considerable amounts of time writing (often 60 minutes or more).
5. Teachers conference with individual students.
6. Writers workshop concludes with a partner or group sharing time.
7. Students generally go through the entire writing process from exploring ideas, writing, editing and revising, to publishing.

What does writers workshop NOT look like?

1. Chaotic or unfocused work time.
2. Assigned topics or formats.

What materials should be used?

Writing folders with expectations, procedures, current pieces of writing, ideas for future writing, spelling checklists, or any other materials that might increase student success.

What do we know about writers workshop?

1. Students become better writers the more they write.
2. Students often write more when self-selecting topics.
3. Teachers can customize instruction to meet the needs of each student.
4. Writers workshop may not prepare students for writing assessments.

Writers Workshop Innovations

1. The procedures can easily be amended to match students' abilities and classroom timelines. Students can collect several pieces of writing and then decide which one they would like to publish. This leads to more time writing and less time publishing.

2. Students' writing samples can be collected in notebooks by mode or genre and made available to other students for future writing ideas.

    EXAMPLE: Mystery stories can be placed in one section of a notebook, nonfiction in another. Then students can read these student-created selections to gain ideas.

3. There are many ways for students to share their writing during the editing/revision process.

    TIP: Students can put out a piece they are working on. Other students can move around the room reading each other's work. Each student leaves a sticky note with a comment. These comments can be focused on a particular skill or more open-ended.

4. Teachers can identify specific skills that would enhance students' writing and then focus mini-lessons on these skills.

    EXAMPLES: Explode the Moment—Students take one particular moment in their writing and rewrite in slow motion, expanding the moment to give the reader incredible detail.

    Snapshots—Students take one particular situation and rewrite as if a "snapshot" or photo had been taken. (Lane, 1993)

5. Students are more likely to write if they have an audience for their writing. There are many ways of getting students' writing published.

Magazines That Publish Student Writing

Chickadee	255 Great Arrow Ave., Buffalo, NY 14207
Children's Digest	100 Waterway Blvd., Indianapolis, IN 46206
Cobblestone	30 Grove St., Peterborough, NH 03458
Creative Kids	100 Pine Ave., Holmes, PA 19043
Cricket	PO Box 51145, Boulder, CO 80323
Kid City	PO Box 51277, Boulder, CO 80322
Merlyn's Pen	98 Main St., East Greenwich, RI 02818
National Geographic World	17th & M Sts. NW, Washington, DC 20036
Ranger Rick	8925 Leesburg Pike, Vienna, VA 22184
Shoe Tree	PO Box 452, Belvidere, NJ 07823
Sports Illustrated for Kids	Time & Life Bldg., Rockefeller Center, NY, NY 10020
Stone Soup	PO Box 83, Santa Cruz, CA 95063
Storyworks	Scholastic, Inc., 555 Broadway, New York, NY 10012
Zillions	PO Box 51777, Boulder, CO 80321

COMPONENT 5

INDEPENDENT WRITING

Definition: Students choose to write on any topic, any format, without teacher monitoring or grading.

Why use independent writing?

Independent writing provides opportunities for students to write for pleasure.

What does independent writing look like?

Students write in journals, notebooks, or on the computer.

What does independent writing NOT look like?

Assigned topics with teachers' grading.

What materials should be used?

Lots of writing samples and books about how other authors became writers or where they obtained their ideas.

> EXAMPLES: Lois Lowry's book *Looking Back: A Book of Memories* (1998) shows students how her own experiences became ideas for her books. Other valuable books include *Shoptalk: Learning to Write With Writers* by Donald Murray (1990) and *Meet the Authors and Illustrators: Volumes 1 and 2* by Deborah Kovacs and James Preller (1999).

What do we know about independent writing?

Many students will self-select to write if given the opportunity. Many authors became writers because they were encouraged to write and given time to write.

Checklist for Components of an Effective, Complete Writing Program

Rate each item on a 1-4 scale.

	Low			High
1. Modeled and interactive writing are used with primary grade students.	1	2	3	4
2. Structured writing instruction aligns to objectives and assessments.	1	2	3	4
3. Writing mini-lessons and instruction are based on students' needs.	1	2	3	4
4. Students are learning to write many different modes and formats.	1	2	3	4
5. Literature and other texts are used as models for writing.	1	2	3	4
6. Students are involved in self-assessing their own writing.	1	2	3	4
7. Students receive meaningful, specific feedback on their writing.	1	2	3	4
8. Students are becoming better writers.	1	2	3	4
9. Students enjoy writing and take pride in their writing.	1	2	3	4

SCORING: Any area scoring below a 3 needs further review.

Copyright © 2004 by Corwin Press. All rights reserved. Reprinted from *The Book of Reading and Writing Ideas, Tips, and Lists for the Elementary Classroom* by Sandra E. Anderson. Thousand Oaks, CA: Corwin Press, www.corwinpress.com. Reproduction authorized only for the local school site that has purchased this book.

Chapter 5
Teaching Writing Skills in Context

Success Story

Sentence variety was lacking in students' writing. Teachers used two approaches—they had students look for interesting sentence structures in the books they were reading, and they taught students to expand and combine sentences taken from their own writing. This led to more interesting, complex sentences in students' writing and improved scores on writing assessments.

Writing skills instruction is most successful if it is taught in context rather than through isolated skill instruction. The essential elements of writing skill instruction include content, the use of language, mechanics, and revision/editing.

Content instruction focuses on the students' ability to communicate their ideas in an organized, clear, and complete way.

The **use of language** includes such things as word choice, sentence completeness and variety, voice, and grammar skills.

Conventions or mechanics includes capitalization, punctuation, and spelling.

Revision and editing demonstrate a re-working of the piece of writing.

The most important factor is that writing skills are taught in the context of reading or writing.

ELEMENT 1

CONTENT INSTRUCTION

Content instruction includes choice of topic, the purpose for the writing, and how best to convey the message. Reading selections can be used as examples of each type of writing, and students' writing samples can be used to determine instructional topics.

What should writing content instruction look like?

1. The primary focus of writing instruction is content.

2. Instruction may be presented to the whole group, small groups, or one-on-one.

3. Many examples will be presented and students will be involved in describing the author's style and craft.

4. Students will write their own pieces.

What should writing content instruction NOT look like?

Unfocused instruction or writing assignments prior to instruction.

What materials should be used?

1. A wide variety of reading materials.

2. Many writing samples.

What do we know about writing instruction focusing on content?

1. Instruction improves students' writing.

2. Reading a wide variety of examples will lead to better writing.

3. Specific feedback improves students' writing.

Content Innovations

1. **Purposes of writing**—Writing instruction can align to state standards and focus on expository, narrative, persuasive, descriptive, procedural, or report writing. Examples of each type of writing can be presented to students. A description or list of criteria can be developed for each type of writing. Students can collect outstanding examples of each type of writing and compare the writing to the criteria. By starting with literary examples, students will be more successful in writing their own pieces.

2. **Organization of the writing**—Students can explore different organizational structures, identify the organization of a piece of writing, collect samples, and select organizational structures for their own writing. Some of these include sequential, chronological, point-by-point analysis, development of the main idea with details, or comparison-contrast.

3. **Genre study**—One way of introducing writing is to have students read different genres such as historical fiction, mysteries, realistic fiction, folk tales, fantasy, science fiction, biographies, memoirs, or informational text. Students identify the key characteristics of a particular genre. Students can then use these key characteristics in their own writing.

4. **Format study**—In addition, students can be shown a variety of formats, including diaries, letters, brochures, editorials, posters, magazine articles, and newspaper articles. As students see what other authors have done, they will begin to incorporate

these ideas into their own writing.

5. **Nonfiction and content area writing**—Students can read several nonfiction pieces on one topic and compare the features, information, and writing style. Students can use these techniques when writing their own nonfiction pieces.

6. **Graphic organizers**—Students can use graphic organizers or visual representations to identify the structure used by the author. Students can then use these same graphic organizers for their writing.

ELEMENT 2

USE OF LANGUAGE

Teachers can provide students with text that highlights innovative ways of using language. If students are asked to focus on the use of language, word choice, sentence fluency, and voice, they will begin to incorporate these techniques into their own writing. Evaluating students' writing is the best way to determine the focus of the instruction.

What should language instruction look like?

1. Teachers will observe students' writing, identify students' needs, and then provide focus lessons in the areas of need.

2. Students will be given models for language structures.

3. Students will read and discuss the different language structures.

4. Students will be encouraged to incorporate these into their own writing and share examples.

5. Teachers will decide if further instruction is necessary.

6. Writing will be shared, discussed, and revised.

What should language instruction NOT look like?

1. Workbook pages.

2. Lessons unrelated to students' writing or reading.

What materials should be used?

Reading materials and writing samples.

What do we know about language instruction?

1. Students who read more, write better.

2. Focused instruction will improve students' writing.

3. Studying how other authors use language leads to improved writing.

Language Usage Innovations

1. **Word choice**—Students can be given outstanding literary examples and discuss the author's choice of words. Students then revise their writing, looking at word choice.

   TIP: Unique words can be replaced with ordinary words. Students can then discuss how the choice of words impacts them as readers. This same activity can be used in reverse where ordinary words are replaced by unique words.

2. **Overused words**—Students can identify overused words and then brainstorm other words that could be used.

   TIP: Following the brainstorming or the collecting of words, students can discuss the subtle differences in the words. These lists or webs of words can be placed on posters around the room or in students' writing folders.

3. **Vocabulary**—Students can locate challenging words and discuss why the author chose these particular words.

   TIP: Students can incorporate some of these words into their own writing. They can also add "mystery words" that may challenge their classmates.

4. **Voice**—Students can evaluate how the writer presented his/her message. As students understand how the writer imparted a personal tone or flavor to the piece, it will help them add their own voice to their writing.

5. **Sentence combining**—Students can be given several short sentences. These can be from a reading selection or teacher prepared. Students can then combine the sentences into longer sentences.

   TIP: Following this activity, students can decide which is better, the shorter sentences or the longer. They can also talk about how the length of the sentence impacts the mood of the writing. As noted earlier, interesting resource materials are William Strong's *Sentence Combining: A Composing Book* (1994) and *Writer's Toolbox: A Sentence Combining Workshop* (1995).

6. **Sentence expansion**—Students can be given short sentences and then can expand the sentences by adding adjectives, adverbs, phrases, clauses, and so on.

   TIP: Early primary reading materials are great sources of short sentences.

7. **Sentence completeness**—Students can be given several complete sentences and several fragments. They can then identify the complete sentences and can write completions for the sentence fragments. These sentences can be taken from students' writing.

8. **Figurative language**—Teachers can collect examples of similes, metaphors, etc. to present to students.

   TIP: In addition, students can collect examples from literary pieces. Notebooks can be created for similes, metaphors, personification, and so on. Students can add to these notebooks by writing their own examples or finding ones written by other authors. These notebooks can be used for reference when students are doing their own writing.

9. **Literary devices**—Reading is ideal for introducing students to a wide variety of literary devices, such as foreshadowing, flashbacks, visual imagery, and so on. Students can then attempt to use these literary devices in their writing. These are great skills for high-achieving students.

10. **Idioms**—Many great books present well-known idioms.

> EXAMPLES: Terban's *In a Pickle and Other Funny Idioms* (1983), *Mad as a Wet Hen! And Other Funny Idioms* (1987), and *Punching the Clock: Funny Action Idioms* (1990) are excellent sources. These are particularly valuable for English as a Second Language students.

ELEMENT 3

MECHANICS

Capitalization and Punctuation

Modeled writing, mini-lessons, and reading are effective ways of introducing and reinforcing capitalization and punctuation.

What should instruction in mechanics look like?

1. Short, focused lessons are best.
2. Topics are selected based on students' needs by evaluating students' writing.
3. Lessons may be for the whole group, small group, or individual. Often topics can be introduced to the entire group but must be followed up in small groups or in individual conferences.
4. Students benefit from writing their own usage rules.

What should the instruction in mechanics NOT look like?

1. An established sequence of skills unrelated to students' needs.
2. Worksheets or practice sheets done in isolation.

What materials should be used?

1. Writing samples.
2. Reading materials.

What do we know about teaching mechanics?

1. Students must see the relevancy for learning to occur.
2. Instruction in mechanics will improve writing.
3. Teaching skills in isolation will not work.

Capitalization and Punctuation Innovations

1. Capitalization—Students can look at reading materials for examples and then write their own rules for capitalization.

   TIP: These rules can be posted in the classroom. Checklists can be created for students' writing folders and can be sent home. As new rules are developed, students can add the new rules to their checklists. Each student can have different rules on his or her list that he or she is being held accountable for.

2. Punctuation—Students can look for different types of punctuation during their reading. A punctuation poster can be created with examples of each.

   TIP: Checklists can be created. When students write, they can identify where they have used each of the punctuation rules. The checklists can be expanded over time.

Spelling

Spelling instruction should be an integral part of students' writing. Spelling words should be selected from students' writing with the focus being on high-utility words—those words used most frequently.

What should spelling instruction look like?

1. Students should practice three to five words per week. These words become basic spelling words. Students are expected to spell these words correctly all the time including in all daily work.

   TIP: Content area words or reading vocabulary words should not be spelling words because they are not generally high-utility words. These words can be posted in the classroom during a particular unit of study for students to reference when writing. Students should be expected to spell the words correctly if they are posted.

2. Students should not practice spelling words incorrectly.

3. Phonics instruction and word walls can reinforce spelling instruction.

   RESOURCE: *Spelling Sourcebook Series* (2002) by Sitton.

What should spelling instruction NOT look like?

1. Weekly spelling lists of 10-20 words.

2. Friday or weekly tests.

3. Students spelling words correctly on a test but incorrectly in daily work.

What materials should be used?

1. High-utility words selected from students' writing.

2. Dry erasable white boards or chalkboards to practice spelling.

3. Manipulatives for students to practice spelling.

What do we know about spelling instruction?

1. Students will not improve unless they are held accountable for the correct spelling.

2. It is better to master high-utility words because they give the most mileage.

3. Emergent readers will use invented or temporary spelling, but by approximately the middle of first grade, students should begin moving toward standard spelling on the words they have been taught.

4. It is hard to unlearn incorrect spelling; therefore, it is better to practice the correct spelling.

5. More than three to five words per week is unmanageable—both for students to learn and teachers to monitor.

6. Multi-syllabic words can be spelled in chunks using the common patterns or rimes.

Spelling Innovations

1. Students can practice words in many different, multi-sensory ways. This might include using Wikki Stix, tracings, sand, white boards, chalk, and so on. The key is, "Is the correct spelling transferring to their writing?"

2. Students can keep "try cards" in their writing folders. They can try the word to see if it "looks right" prior to writing it. After writing the word on the "try card," students can have someone check the spelling.

3. Students can create sentences for homonyms and keep these for reference. These can also be displayed in the classroom.

4. Students can practice proofreading skills by identifying words that look wrong.

ELEMENT 4

REVISING AND EDITING

Revision and editing are difficult skills to teach. Students often prefer to "be done." Yet, to improve the quality of their writing, students need to be taught revision and editing skills. Students should revise and edit any piece of writing that is going to be published.

What should revision and editing instruction look like?

1. Revision and editing should be taught in small increments.

2. Students should evaluate their own writing, looking for a few particular items.

3. Students need to demonstrate and prove how they have revised or edited their work.

4. Peer editing may be an effective part of the revision and editing process.

What should revision and editing instruction NOT look like?

1. Skills not relevant to students' writing.

2. The teacher doing the revising and editing (unless with very young writers).

What materials should be used?

Student's writing and other unedited writings.

What do we know about teaching revision and editing?

1. Students get better if they receive focused instruction.

2. Students will revise and edit if is a high priority in the classroom.

Revision Innovations

1. Individual student-teacher conferences can focus on editing or revision.

   TIP: It is critical with young or struggling writers that the focus be on content first, mechanics later.

2. Peers can encourage content revision through questioning strategies.

   TIP: Students can read each other's papers and write 1-2 questions they have on sticky notes. The key is that they are only writing questions they have about the content—they are not criticizing. If several students read one selection, the writer receives numerous questions about the content of the writing—what was unclear, what didn't make sense, what elaborations might help.

   RESOURCE: Barry Lane's book, *After the End: Teaching and Learning Creative Revision* (1993) provides many ideas for revision.

Writing skills instruction is most effective when students' needs are identified, instruction is presented in the context of reading and writing, and students have multiple opportunities to write, receiving specific feedback.

Checklist for Teaching Writing Skills in Context

Rate each item on a 1-4 scale.

	Low			High
1. Literature and writing samples are used as models for writing.	1	2	3	4
2. Writing skills instruction is based on students' needs.	1	2	3	4
3. Writing content is the top priority.	1	2	3	4
4. Students review and discuss how other authors use language.	1	2	3	4
5. Students are exposed to a variety of genres and formats.	1	2	3	4
6. Students are held accountable for grammar skills that have been taught.	1	2	3	4
7. Students are held accountable for spelling words that have been taught.	1	2	3	4
8. Students have multiple opportunities to write.	1	2	3	4
9. Revision and editing are a part of the writing process.	1	2	3	4
10. Students self-assess their writing.	1	2	3	4
11. Teachers conference with individual students.	1	2	3	4
12. Specific feedback is provided.	1	2	3	4
13. Students take pride in their writing.	1	2	3	4
14. Students are improving in content, use of language, and mechanics.	1	2	3	4

SCORING: Any area scoring below a 3 needs further review.

Copyright © 2004 by Corwin Press. All rights reserved. Reprinted from *The Book of Reading and Writing Ideas, Tips, and Lists for the Elementary Classroom* by Sandra E. Anderson. Thousand Oaks, CA: Corwin Press, www.corwinpress.com. Reproduction authorized only for the local school site that has purchased this book.

Chapter 6
Other Instructional Factors Impacting the Success of Reading and Writing Programs

> **Success Story**
>
> *An elementary school inventoried its instructional materials and decided that it needed many more sets of fiction and nonfiction books if it was to entice students to read. Innovative ways were sought to fund these text sets, including reducing the amount of money spent on consumables, soliciting financial support from local businesses, seeking financial assistance from the parent-teacher-student association, using bonus points, holding book fairs, looking for discounted titles, and providing purchase ideas to parents. Within one year the school had 30 additional sets of titles per grade level, and students were reading more with greater enthusiasm.*

A successful literacy program must take several other factors into consideration:

- The use of **instructional time**

- The quantity and quality of **instructional materials**

- The use of a **print-rich environment**

- The use of a **wide variety of assessments**

All of these impact students' reading and writing performance.

FACTOR 1

INSTRUCTIONAL TIME

How much time should be spent in reading and writing? The use of instructional time must be maximized to strengthen students' performance in reading and writing.

1. Research is showing that ideally **90-120 minutes** per day should be spent in **reading instruction**, not counting minutes spent on read alouds or silent reading (Taylor, Pearson, Clark, and Walpole, 2000).

2. Another **60 minutes** should be spent on **writing**.

3. The goal for **independent reading** should be **15-30 minutes** per day.

    TIP: Reading and writing time can be maximized by eliminating interruptions. When evaluated the average classroom interruption took 3 minutes per interruption, and there were 10 interruptions per day. This equals 15 days per year.

    TIP: Evaluate how much time is spent taking tests or practicing for tests and then recoup some instructional time. In a major survey teachers were asked how much time was spent practicing for or taking tests—from this data, the survey determined that an average of 33.7 days per school year was spent on practicing or taking tests. This is valuable time that could be used for reading and writing instruction.

Instructional time must be maximized if students are to improve in reading and writing.

FACTOR 2

INSTRUCTIONAL MATERIALS

Teachers and students need access to many, many books and other reading materials. They also need a variety of different types of materials, including books of different levels, genres, and formats.

    TIP: Kindergarten and first-grade students should read four or more books per day; second-grade students should read four or more small books or one to two chapters per day; and students in Grades 3 to 6 should read a minimum of 30 books per year. Therefore, teachers and students must have access to a large quantity of reading materials.

    CONSIDERATION: If students are spending two hours per day reading, they will need to have more than basal anthologies. If students read an anthology 20-30 minutes per day, they would read the entire book in 18-20 hours or approximately 40 days. If students read for 90 minutes they could read the entire anthology in three weeks.

Ideal Classroom Materials List

1. Leveled Reading Books

Each classroom should have access to sets of leveled reading books for guided reading. It is important that class materials be leveled so that students can read materials on their instructional levels. When matching books to students, the following guidelines need to be taken into consideration:

Materials for Emergent and Early Readers

Large font size and large spaces between words

Limited number of words

One line per page

Consistency of text placement

Illustrations support the text

Repetition of language patterns

Predictable text

Writing that more closely matches oral language

Materials for Developing Readers

Book length increases

Character development and plot become more complex

Concepts are age appropriate

Text is not as predictable

Fewer illustrations

Placement of text varies on page

Return sweep is necessary

Students have some familiarity with topic

Dialogue begins to appear

Materials for More Fluent Readers

Themes are more sophisticated

Literary or figurative language appears

Content is age appropriate

Material is of interest to students

Sentences become more complex

Vocabulary consists of multisyllabic words

Books increase in length and include chapters

There are few illustrations and they may not match the text

Greater variety of genres and formats

RESOURCE: *Better Books! Better Readers!: How to Choose, Use, and Level Books for Children in the Primary Grades* (1999) by Hart-Hewins, Wells, and Stratton.

2. Sets of Reading Books for Literature Circles

Each classroom should have access to sets of reading books for literature circles. There are thousands of book titles available for book sets that can be used for literature circles. Some considerations include: topics of interest to your students, appropriateness for your community, balance of genre, balance of fiction and nonfiction, and the teacher's enthusiasm for the books. Some favorite titles or series are listed below. The most recent publication date has been used.

Grades 1 and 2 Series Books for Fluent Readers

Junie B. Jones by Park. Random House, 1997.

Julian Stories by Cameron. Random House, 1989.

Frog and Toad by Lobel. HarperCollins, 1984.

Nate the Great by Sharmat. Young Yearling, 1977.

The Boxcar Children by Warner. Albert Whitman, 1989.

Marvin Redpost by Sachar. Random House, 1992.

Riverside Kids by Hurwitz. HarperTrophy, 2001.

Polk Street School by Giff. Young Yearling, 1989.

Grades 3 and 4 Trade Books

Fourth Floor Twins by Adler. Viking Press, 1986.

Fantastic Mr. Fox by Dahl. Puffin, 1998.

Be a Perfect Person in Just Three Days by Manes. Houghton Mifflin, 1996.

Owls in the Family by Mowat. Laureleaf, 1996.

The Dog Who Wouldn't Be by Mowat. Bantam, 1984.

The Lucky Stone by Clifton. Yearling Books, 1986.

Ramona by Cleary. Scott, Foresman, 1992.

How to Eat Fried Worms by Rockwell. Yearling Books, 1953.

Cricket in Times Square by Selden. Random House, 1970.

Mr. Popper's Penguins by Atwater. Little, Brown & Co., 1988.

Babe the Gallant Pig by King-Smith. Bt Bound, 1997.

Cam Jansen Mysteries by Adler. Puffin, 1997.

Frindle by Clements. Aladdin, 1998.

Encyclopedia Brown by Sobol. Bantam Skylark, 1993

Wayside School by Sachar. Avon, 1998.

Maniac Magee by Spinelli. Little, Brown & Co., 2000.

The Stories Huey Tells by Cameron. Young Yearling, 1997.

Ida Early Comes Over the Mountains by Burch. Bt Bound, 1999.

Grades 5 and 6 Trade Books

The Search for Delicious by Babbitt. Farrar, Straus & Giroux, 1991.

Tuck Everlasting by Babbitt. Farrar, Straus & Giroux, 1986.

The Midnight Fox by Byars. Scott, Foresman, 1996.

From the Mixed-Up Files of Mrs. Basil E. Frankweiler by Konigsburg. Yearling Books, 1977.

The Great Brain by Fitzgerald. Bt Bound, 1999.

Island of the Blue Dolphins by O'Dell. Random House,

The Cay by Taylor. Yearling Books, 2002.

Great Gilly Hopkins by Paterson. HarperCollins, 1978.

The Sign of the Beaver by Speare. Yearling Books, 1994.

Castle in the Attic by Winthrop. Yearling Books, 1986.

Julie of the Wolves by George. HarperTrophy, 1974.

One-Eyed Cat by Fox. Aladdin, 2000.

Hatchet by Paulsen. Pocket Books, 1999.

White Mountains by Christopher. Pocket Books, 1999.

Advanced

Westmark by Alexander. AlloyBooks, 2002.

The Westing Game by Raskin. Scott, Foresman, 1997.

Wolves of Willoughby Chase by Aiken. Yearling Books, 1987.

Wrinkle in Time by L'Engle. Yearling Books, 1973.

My Brother Sam Is Dead by Collier. Scholastic, 1989.

Z for Zachariah by O'Brien. Pocket Books, 1987.

Roll of Thunder, Hear My Cry by Taylor. Puffin, 1991.

The Curse of the Blue Figurine by Bellairs. Bt Bound, 1996.

Homesick by Fritz. Paper Star, 1999.

The Dark is Rising by Cooper. Aladdin, 1999.

The House of Dies Drear by Hamilton. Pocket Books, 1984.

The Watsons Go to Birmingham by Curtis. Random House, 1997.

The Root Cellar by Lunn. Puffin, 1996.

Redwall by Jacques. Ace, 1998.

Farewell to Manzanar by Houston. Bantam, 1983.

3. Books for Independent Reading

Each classroom should have a minimum of 300 different titles on a variety of levels for independent reading. It is important to teach students how to select books at their independent reading level. Students will not improve if they are reading at their frustration level. During guided reading students should be at their instructional level, but during self-selected reading they should be reading at their independent level.

The levels are defined as follows:

> **Frustration:** word recognition below 90% and a lack of comprehension
>
> **Instructional:** word recognition between 90-94% with comprehension
>
> **Independent:** word recognition at or above 95% with comprehension

How can students be taught to self-select the appropriate books? One strategy is to use the Goldilocks method—they are looking for books that are not too hard, not too easy, but just right.

Questions to identify TOO HARD:

Do you have trouble understanding the book?

Are many of the words too difficult?

Do you need to ask for help?

Is it slow reading?

Questions to identify TOO EASY:

Can you read it very smoothly and quite quickly?

Do you know all the words?

Questions to identify JUST RIGHT:

Do you understand what you have read?

Do you know most of the words?

Can you read with little or no help?

---

4. Access to Books of Various Genres

Each classroom needs access to a variety of genres including:

autobiographies	biographies	diaries	fantasy	fables
historical fiction	folk tales	mysteries	legends	memoirs
expository texts	myths	plays	poetry	realistic fiction
science fiction	tall tales	traditional tales		

5. Printed Materials in a Variety of Formats

Each classroom needs a variety of formats including:

advertisements	almanacs	atlases	brochures	cartoons
classified ads	comics	directions	editorials	journals
letters	magazines	manuals	memos	newspapers
poems	songs			

6. Different Versions of the Same Story

Different versions of the same story line are a great way of including multi-cultural books, capturing the interest of students, challenging higher-level readers, providing opportunities for struggling readers to reread familiar materials, developing fluency, and teaching compare and contrast.

Cinderella Theme

Yeh-shen by L. Ai-ling. Philomel, 1982.

Moss Gown by W. Hooks. Clarion, 1987.

Princess Furball by C. Huck. Greenwillow, 1989.

Mufaro's Beautiful Daughters by J. Steptoe. Lothrop, Lee, & Shepard, 1987.

Vasilisa the Beautiful by T. Whitney. Macmillan, 1970.

Cinder Edna by E. Jackson. Lothrop, 1994.

Cinderella by A. Ehrlich. Dial, 1985.

Cinderella by R. Innocenti. Creative Education, 1983.

Sidney Rella and the Glass Sneaker by B. Myers. Macmillan, 1985.

The Korean Cinderella by S. Climo. HarperCollins, 1993.

The Egyptian Cinderella by S. Climo. Crowell, 1989.

Prince Cinders by B. Cole. Putnam, 1987.

Cinder-Elly by F. Minters. Viking, 1994.

That Awful Cinderella by A. Granowsky. Steck-Vaughn, 1993.

Cinderella Bigfoot by M. Thaler. Scholastic, 1997.

Jack and the Beanstalk Theme

Jim and the Beanstalk by R. Briggs. Coward-McCann, 1970.

Jack and the Beanstalk by L.B. Cauley. G. P. Putnam, 1983.

Jack the Giant-Killer by B.S. DeRegniers. Atheneum, 1987.

The History of Mother Twaddle and the Marvelous Achievements of Her Son Jack by J. Harris. Seabury Press, 1974.

Jack and the Bean Tree by G. Haley. Crown, 1986.

Jack and the Beanstalk by T. Ross. Delacorte Press, 1980.

Jack and the Beanstalk See & Say Storybook by Suzy-Jane Tanner. Award Publications, 1987.

Jack and the Beanstalk by P. Galdone. Clarion, 1974.

Janie and the Giant by S. Barchas. Scholastic, 1977.

Rapunzel Theme

Petrosinella by G. Basil. Frederick Warne, 1981.

Rapunzel by J. Grimm & W. Grimm. Creative Education, 1984.

Rapunzel by B. Rogasky. Holiday House, 1982.

Red Riding Hood Theme

Little Red Riding Hood by J. Grimm & W. Grimm. Scholastic, 1971.

Flossie & the Fox by P. McKissack. Dial, 1986.

Lon Po Po by E. Young. Philomel, 1989.

The Three Little Pigs Theme

The Three Little Pigs by P. Galdone. Seabury Press, 1970.

The True Story of the Three Little Pigs by J. Scieszka. Viking Kestrel, 1989.

The Three Little Javelinas by S. Lowell. Rising Moon, 1992.

The Three Little Hawaiian Pigs and the Magic Shark by D. Laird. Barnaby, 1990.

The Three Little Cajun Pigs by B. Amoss. MTC Press, 1999.

The Three Little Pigs and the Fox: An Appalachian Tale by W. Hooks. Aladdin, 1997.

7. Nonfiction Books

Each classroom should have access to single copies or guided reading sets for teaching nonfiction or expository text structures. Expository texts have unique characteristics, and students will benefit from instruction on these unique features. Content area materials may be used for teaching nonfiction text structures.

Organizational Structures

Content area books typically model each of these five different organizational structures:

- Description
- Sequence
- Compare/contrast
- Cause and effect
- Problem/solution

Informational Text Features

- **Print Features:** Varying fonts, bold print, colored print, bullets, titles, headings, subheadings, italics, labels, and captions

- **Graphic Aids:** Diagrams, sketches, graphs, figures, maps, charts, tables, cross-sections, timelines, overlays, flow charts, inserts, and excerpts of original documents

- **Organizational Aids:** Table of contents, index, glossary, preface, pronunciation guide, appendix, vocabulary in margin, sources, footnotes

- **Illustrations:** Maps, photographs, drawings, paintings, scale, close ups, bird's-eye views, and perspectives

Sources of Nonfiction Leveled Books	
Benchmark	1-877-236-2465
Mondo	1-888-886-6636
National Geographic	1-800-368-2728
Newbridge	1-800-867-0307
Rigby	1-800-822-8661
Scholastic	1-800-325-6149
The Wright Group	1-800-523-2371

8. Books That Feature Literary Devices

Each teacher should have access to single copies of books that teach literary devices. This chart provides a list of books that are particularly effective for teaching these literary devices.

Alliteration Repetition of initial sounds in two or more words.	*Prince Cinders* by B. Cole. Putnam, 1987. *Feathers and Fools* by Mem Fox. Harcourt Brace, 1996. *A My Name Is Alice* by Jane Bayer and Steven Kellogg. Dial, 1992.
Flashback Events that happened before the time of the current narration; some authors use memories or dreams as flashbacks.	*Miss Rumphius* by B. Cooney. Viking, 1982. *Grandfather's Journey* by A. Say. Houghton Mifflin, 1993. *The Wreck of the Zephyr* by C. Van Allsburg. Houghton Mifflin, 1983.
Foreshadowing A clue that the author gives that something is about to happen.	*The Patchwork Quilt* by V. Flournoy. Dial, 1985. *The Stranger* by C. Van Allsburgh. Houghton Mifflin, 1986.
Inference Drawing conclusions from the information that is given.	*Rose Blanche* by R. Innocenti & C. Gallaz. Stewart, Talbori & Chang, 1990. *Ben's Trumpet* by R. Isadora. Greenwillow, 1979. *The Garden of Abdul Gasazi* by C. Van Allsburg. Houghton Mifflin, 1979.
Metaphor Comparison between two unlike things to show similarity; implies that one thing is the other.	*The Rough-Face Girl* by R. Martin. G. P. Putnam, 1992. *The Tale of the Mandarin Ducks* by K. Paterson. Lodestar, 1990. *Greyling* by J. Yolen. Philomel, 1991.
Onomatopoeia Formation of a word to imitate or suggest the sound of the word, e.g. buzz.	*Smoky Night* by E. Bunting. Harcourt Brace, 1994. *Sky Dogs* by J. Yolen. Harcourt Brace, 1990.

Point of View Seeing the circumstances through another's eye.	*Bella Arabella* by L. Fosburgh. Macmillan, 1985. *Woof* by A. Ahlberg. Viking Kestrel, 1986. *The Wall* by E. Bunting. Clarion, 1990. *The True Story of the Three Little Pigs* by J. Scieszka. Viking, 1989.
Simile A comparison between two unlike things to show similarity; a simile implies that one thing is like another.	*Two Mrs. Gibsons* by T. Igus. Children's Book Press, 1996. *The Whale's Song* by D. Sheldon. Dial, 1991. *Nettie's Trip South* by A. Turner. Macmillan, 1987.
Symbolism Something that is itself and also represents something else.	*Fly Away Home* by E. Bunting. Clarion, 1991. *The Lotus Seed* by S. Garland. Harcourt Brace, 1993. *The Rag Coat* by L. Mills. Little, Brown, 1991. *Pink and Say* by P. Polacco. Philomel, 1994. *The Butterfly* by P. Polacco. Philomel, 2000. *Rumpelstiltskin's Daughter* by D. Stanley. Morrow, 1994.

Some titles taken from "Picture Books Containing Examples of Literary Devices" by Cyndi Giorgis and Judy Pollak, *English Journal*, 88(4), 31-33.

9. Outstanding Books That Model Writing Styles and Skills

Each teacher should have available single copies of outstanding books for teaching structured writing and writing skills. Picture books can be effectively used as models for the traits of writing for both primary and intermediate students. The following are some titles worthy of consideration:

Ideas—the content or message

The Cactus Flower Bakery by H. Allard. Harper, 1991.

Everybody Needs a Rock by B. Baylor. Macmillan, 1974.

Miss Rumphius by B. Cooney. Viking Penguin, 1982.

Wilfrid Gordon McDonald Partridge by M. Fox. Kane-Miller, 1985.

Chrysanthemum by K. Henkes. Greenwillow, 1991.

Frederick by L. Lionni. Random House, 1967.

Roxaboxen by A. McLaren. Scott, Foresman, 1992.

The Butterfly by P. Polacco. Philomel, 2000.

Organization—the structure

This Quiet Lady by C. Zolotow. HarperCollins, 2000.

Letters From Rifka by K. Hesse. Puffin, 1993.

Why Mosquitoes Buzz in People's Ears by V. Aardema. Dial, 1975.

Who Is This Beast? By K. Baker. Harcourt Brace, 1990.

The Mitten by Jan Brett. G. P. Putnam, 1989.

Good Dog, Carl by A. Day. Green Tiger Press, 1984.

Possum Magic by M. Fox. Harcourt Brace, 1983.

My Prairie Year by B. Harvey. Holiday House, 1986.

The Snowy Day by E. J. Keats. Penguin, 1962.

Lizard's Song by G. Shannon. Greenwillow, 1981.

Alexander and the Terrible, Horrible, No Good Very Bad Day by
    J. Viorst. Macmillan, 1972.

A Chair for My Mother by V. Williams. Greenwillow, 1982.

Voice—the tone

The Jolly Postman or Other People's Letters by J. & A. Ahlberg. Little, Brown, &
    Co., 1991.

Miss Nelson Has a Field Day by H. Allard. Houghton Mifflin, 1985.

Smoky Night by E. Bunting. Harcourt Brace, 1994.

The Wall by E. Bunting. Clarion, 1990.

The Legend of the Blue Bonnet by T. DePaola. G. P. Putnam, 1983.

Tough Boris by M. Fox. Harcourt Brace, 1994.

Anansi and the Moss-Covered Rock by E. Kimmel. Holiday House, 1988.

Flossie and the Fox by P. McKissack. Dial, 1986.

Martha Speaks by S. Meddaugh. Houghton Mifflin, 1992.

The Paper Bag Princess by Robert Munsch. Annick Press, 1980.

Officer Buckle and Gloria by Peggy Rathman. G. P. Putnam, 1995.

The Frog Prince Continued by J. Scieszka. Viking, 1991.

Two Bad Ants by C. Van Allsburg. Houghton Mifflin, 1988.

Sleeping Ugly by J. Yolen. Paper Star, 1997.

Word Choice—the vocabulary

I Am Really a Princess by C. Shields. Puffin, 1996.

In the Small, Small Pond by D. Fleming. Holt, 1993.

Lunch by D. Fleming. Holt, 1992.

Night Noises by M. Fox. Trumpet, 1989.

Box Turtle at Long Pond by W. George. Greenwillow, 1989.

Many Luscious Lollipops by R. Heller. Putnam & Grosset, 1989.

Antics by C. Hepworth. Trumpet, 1993.

Victor and Christabel by P. Mathers. Knopf, 1993.

Thundercake by P. Polacco. Philomel, 1990.

Clever Tom and the Leprechaun by L. Shute. Scholastic, 1988.

Amos and Boris by W. Steig. Puffin, 1971.

Sentence Fluency—the language structure or rhythm of the language

Amigo by B. Baylor. Macmillan, 1963.

Jamberry by B. Degen. Harper & Row, 1983.

Knoxville, Tennessee by N. Giovanni. Scholastic, 1995.

Daydreamers by E. Greenfield. Dial, 1981.

North Country Night by D. San Souci. Doubleday, 1990.

Caleb & Kate by W. Steig. Farrar, Straus & Giroux, 1977.

Fox's Dream by Tejima. Philomel, 1985.

Conventions—the mechanical correctness

Time to Get Out of the Baths, Shirley by J. Burningham. Crowell, 1978.

Hattie and the Fox by M. Fox. Trumpet, 1986.

Yo! Yes? by C. Raschka. Scholastic, 1993.

FACTOR 3

USING A PRINT-RICH ENVIRONMENT

A print-rich environment can be part of the teaching materials in the classroom. It also provides support to students as they become more effective readers and writers. In addition, if students are involved in creating a print-rich environment, it helps to establish a community of learners and a sense of belonging.

Possible Elements of a Print-Rich Environment

1. **Wall stories**—Students create an innovation of a familiar book, and pages are posted around the classroom.

2. **Bulletin boards**—Bulletin boards are created by students to reinforce skills being taught.

3. **Poetry or song charts**—Poems and songs are written on charts and hung in the classroom.

4. **Word walls**—Word walls are created as reference tools for students. These may include high-frequency words, ABC word walls, onsets and rimes, or any other word wall that will help students. Multi-syllabic words may be used for intermediate students.

5. **Student work**—Students' work can be used as a part of the instructional program.

    TIP: Have students label their work with the goals that have been accomplished.

6. **Reference charts**—Posters of rules or procedures are created so students can refer to them. These may include grammar rules or classroom rules.

7. **Copy search posters**—Posters created by students where they note outstanding literary devices such as great openers or metaphors.

8. **Murals**—Art and text can focus on a content area or literature area.

    TIP: High-achieving students can extend the content of the mural.

9. **Story sequences**—Stories are sequenced and hung in the room. This works well for read alouds where students create summaries of each chapter to hang up around the room.

10. **Modeled writing charts**—Examples of modeled writing can be hung in room for reading practice.

11. **Timelines**—Timelines can be created to provide a sense of organization. This is effective for social studies and for literary pieces where understanding the sequence of events is important.

    TIP: This is particularly effective with complex read alouds where it is important to keep track of the events.

12. **Graphic organizers**—Students can complete a graphic organizer. It can be enlarged and then posted as a model.

> TIP: Keep a file of blank organizers that match the ones posted and encourage students to use these graphic organizers as prewriting strategies.

13. **Pocket charts**—known poems or stories can be sequenced in the pocket chart. Primary students can match sentence strips to picture clues. Intermediate can sequence story events, directions, timeline events, step-by-step procedures, or poems.

14. **Overhead projectors** can be used with transparencies of familiar materials for reading practice.

> TIP: Students enjoy reading transparencies; this is a great way to build fluency.

15. **Content area vocabulary**—lists of content area words can be posted for students' reference.

> TIP: Have students provide illustrations and examples.

16. **Real-life literacy**—create an area for literacy materials around a common theme such as dining options, grocery stores, social services, travel agencies, theaters, museums, or any other relevant theme. Students love to collect and read items.

17. **Clues**—post clues for solving a mystery. This can be a class mystery or a read aloud mystery. Posting the clues helps students keep track of the clues, provides additional reading, and leads students to solving the mystery.

FACTOR 4

INCORPORATING A VARIETY OF ASSESSMENTS

Assessment should be a part of daily instruction focusing on identifying students' instructional needs. A wide variety of assessments should be used, with most of the information being informal and being gathered by the teacher. Assessment should align to instruction—it is critical that students not be tested on information that has not been taught or tested in an unknown format. Assessment should provide information for planning and modifying instruction. Some of the different types of assessments that could be utilized include the following categories:

Reading Assessments

1. **Concepts of Print**

   Used with emergent readers to see if they understand such items as where to start reading.

2. **Phonemic Awareness Tests**

   Used to assess phonemic awareness knowledge and to plan instruction.

3. **Phonics Tests**

Used to assess students' knowledge of the sounds of the alphabet and/or onsets and rimes.

4. **Non-Decodable Word Test**

Used to assess knowledge of non-decodable words.

5. **Running Records**

A running record of students' reading that assesses decoding, sight word knowledge, fluency, and ability to self-correct. Running records can be used to match students to leveled books.

6. **Timed Passages**

The number of words in a passage can be identified and then students can be timed to determine speed of reading. Primary students will read 60-85 wpm, and intermediate students will read approximately 100-200 wpm. Silent reading will be faster than oral reading.

7. **Story Retelling**

Students retell what they have read; this can be used to assess comprehension. This is effective with developing and fluent readers. Usually there is little to retell at the emergent stage.

8. **After-Reading Strategies**

After-reading strategies are selected based on their alignment to the skills being taught and can be used as comprehension measures.

9. **Anecdotal Notes**

As the teacher listens to individual students read, the teacher notes strengths and areas needing additional instruction.

10. **Checklists**

A checklist of skills is developed. The teacher records activities or behaviors observed and plans instruction for those areas not mastered.

11. **Informal Reading Inventories**

Informal reading inventories are leveled passages that are primarily used for placement decisions or when documenting progress. They can be used to assess decoding, fluency, and comprehension.

12. **Reading Interviews**

Teacher conducts student interviews and evaluates and assesses students' knowledge, understanding, and attitudes toward reading.

13. **Criterion-Referenced Tests**

Specific skills tests that can be used to assess individual skill knowledge. Teachers must be sure the skills transfer to "real" reading.

14. **Standards-Based Assessments**

Teachers assess students' achievement of state or district standards. Often the results are delayed and there is little individual student information, so these may or may not provide help with instructional planning.

15. **Standardized Tests**

These are primarily used to judge school or classroom performance. Ideally, standardized tests align to curriculum and instruction. Often they provide very limited information for instructional purposes.

Writing Assessments

1. **Writing Samples**

Students writing samples are evaluated on a ongoing basis to help the teacher make decisions regarding instruction and mini-lessons. These can also show progress over time.

2. **Rubrics**

Rubrics are the expectations for assignments. The criteria can be developed by teachers and/or students and are used to evaluate students' writings. Often the scale is 0 to 5 for each category, and students receive points based on how close they came to the criteria.

TIP: This is one way of clarifying the specific expectations and scoring students in each area. For example, a student can get a 5 for creativity, but a 3 for conventions.

3. **Moderation Panel**

One student's work is collected and a group of teachers review the work. The teachers identify strengths as well as make recommendations about future instruction.

4. **Writing to Prompts**

Students are provided a writing prompt. These are generally used for state assessments. They may provide some instructional information if results are received in a timely way and individual data are provided.

CAUTION: The quality of the writing prompt can have a dramatic impact on student performance.

5. **Spelling**

Daily writing rather than weekly spelling tests is the best measure of assessing spelling performance and identifying needed instruction.

Student Self-Assessments

1. **Rubrics**

As noted above, rubrics are established criteria or expectations. They can be developed with students prior to an assignment and then used by both the teacher and student to evaluate progress in meeting goals.

2. **Narrative**

Students evaluate their own success and develop future goals.

> TIP: This works well if students are specifically asked to identify one or two things they did well and one or two skills they need to work on.

3. **Checklists**

Students use a checklist to evaluate their work quality, participation, or any other criteria.

> TIP: The checklists will be most effective if students have to provide a specific example of their accomplishments.

4. **Journals**

Students write about challenges, difficulties, or how they felt about tasks.

Parent Assessments

1. **Reflections**

Parents comment about their student's learning.

2. **Surveys**

Parents participate in school or classroom surveys regarding the reading and writing program.

3. **Interviews**

Parents are interviewed regarding the reading and writing program.

QUESTIONS TO ASK REGARDING ASSESSMENT

1. Are we assessing essential/critical areas?
2. Are we using the assessment data effectively?
3. Do our assessments align to our instruction?
4. Are the assessments helpful? Are they fair and equitable? Are the results accurate?
5. What is the stress level during assessments?
6. Are we putting too much weight on one or two measures?
7. Are assessment data being used to evaluate teachers? If so, what does this do to morale? To quality of teaching? To desire to work with difficult students? To collaboration among teachers?
8. Are we spending too much time on assessments and too little time on instruction?
9. Do we need more data? If so, in what area?

Checklist for Other Factors Impacting Reading and Writing Programs

Rate each item on a 1-4 scale.

	Low			High
1. Instructional time is being maximized.	1	2	3	4
2. Interruptions are minimized.	1	2	3	4
3. Ninety minutes or more per day is spent on reading.	1	2	3	4
4. Sixty minutes or more per day is spent on writing.	1	2	3	4
5. Twenty to thirty minutes per day is spent on independent reading.	1	2	3	4
6. Adequate leveled materials are available for guided reading.	1	2	3	4
7. Sets of materials are available for literature circles.	1	2	3	4
8. Books of different genres and formats are available.	1	2	3	4
9. Single copies of books are available as examples for writing instruction.	1	2	3	4
10. A print-rich environment is used for classroom instruction.	1	2	3	4
11. Many different types of assessments are utilized.	1	2	3	4
12. Assessment is used to plan instruction.	1	2	3	4

SCORING: Any area scoring below a 3 needs further review.

Copyright © 2004 by Corwin Press. All rights reserved. Reprinted from *The Book of Reading and Writing Ideas, Tips, and Lists for the Elementary Classroom* by Sandra E. Anderson. Thousand Oaks, CA: Corwin Press, www.corwinpress.com. Reproduction authorized only for the local school site that has purchased this book.

Chapter 7
Meeting the Needs of Struggling Readers

> **Success Story**
>
> *An elementary school sought creative ways of meeting the needs of first-grade struggling readers and came up with teaming the communication disorder specialist, the special education teacher, and the reading specialist. The three educators went into the first-grade classrooms for one hour a week. By working with small groups of students on a consistent basis, they were better able to understand students' needs as well as significantly strengthen students' reading performance.*

Struggling readers need additional support, the highest quality of instruction, and materials on their instructional level. Often the instruction that struggling readers receive is quite different from that for good readers.

Areas of Consideration for Struggling Readers	
Challenges	**Solutions**
They are more likely to be reading material that is at the frustration level and too difficult for them.	It is critical that they read leveled materials on their instructional level.
They are more likely to be asked to read aloud even when it is obvious they are struggling.	Solutions include having students read silently first for practice, having students read to another person prior to reading aloud in a group, and monitoring to ensure that struggling readers are reading instructional-level materials. *(Continued)*

Areas of Consideration for Struggling Readers *(Continued)*	
Challenges	**Solutions**
They are more likely to be interrupted when they miscall a word and more likely to be asked to sound out the word.	It is critical that struggling readers consistently be asked, "Did that make sense?" prior to being asked to "Sound it out." In addition, it is important to wait to see if the student self-corrects. This will build greater independence rather than teacher dependence.
They are more likely to pause and wait for the teacher to give them the word.	They should be encouraged to problem solve by being asked what would make sense.

Safety Nets That Make a Difference for Struggling Readers

What do we know about the most effective safety nets?

The most effective safety nets are those that are "home grown" or customized to meet the needs of the individual school and its students. The following is a list of considerations that can make a difference for struggling readers.

SAFETY NET 1

EFFECTIVE TEACHERS

Teachers are the most critical element of any program. Do staff members have the training they need to meet the needs of struggling readers? Are the following being taken into consideration?

A. Matching the most knowledgeable teachers with the most needy students.

B. Ensuring that struggling readers have a limited number of teachers.

> EXAMPLE: When evaluating a struggling reader, it was discovered that the student, who had trouble adapting to change, had seven different teachers every day. His schedule was changed to minimize the number of different people he had to deal with, and his performance and behavior improved.

C. Placing struggling readers with teachers who have outstanding classroom management skills.

D. Using instructional strategies and prompts that align to students' needs.

> TIP: These four reflective questions have been valuable for teachers: To what extent are my students engaged in higher-level thinking during discussions about the text? To what extent are my students engaged in active versus passive responding during reading lessons? To what extent am I teaching reading with a student-support stance (coaching-modeling) in addition to a teacher-directed stance? To what extent am I teaching reading strategies in addition to reading skills (Taylor, 2003)?

E. Modeling reading and writing through strategies such as think alouds where teachers explain their own thinking process as they read and write.

F. Creating a community of learners where risk taking, positive attitudes, feelings of acceptance, and respect are present.

SAFETY NET 2

OUTSTANDING CLASSROOM INSTRUCTION

Outstanding classroom instruction is absolutely essential for struggling readers. Is classroom instruction taking into consideration the needs of struggling readers? Are all of the following included?

A. High expectations for struggling students.

B. Teacher modeling and using think alouds to help struggling students understand what is going on when others read.

C. Alignment of curriculum, instruction, and assessment.

D. Using a wide variety of instructional strategies or differentiating instruction.

D. Engaging students in the learning by establishing personal connections and encouraging higher-level thinking.

E. Active involvement including physical movement and role playing.

F. Frequent monitoring with specific feedback.

> TIP: Struggling readers often do not know how they are doing and do not see their improvement. Clear feedback can be provided by charting each student's improvement, involving students in self-evaluation, and incorporating specific teacher praise.

G. Encouraging literate conversations.

SAFETY NET 3

EFFECTIVE READING INSTRUCTION

Effective reading instruction is critical. What are the characteristics of effective reading instruction for struggling readers? Are all of these included?

A. **Instructional-level materials** are used for reading—90-94% accuracy with comprehension.

B. **Word study**—Struggling readers are generally weak in this area and will benefit from 10-15 minutes per day of intensive instruction on word study. Based upon students' needs, this instruction may include any or all of the following:

- *Phonemic awareness*—Struggling readers are often uncomfortable playing with the sounds of language.

  TIP: Provide jump rope jingles, raps, songs, and chants to encourage students to listen for the sounds.

- *Phonics*—Onsets and rimes provide the greatest boost in reading.

  TIP: Word walls are effective in helping the struggling reader to generalize about the rime patterns. One example of each of the patterns is placed on the wall and when students are having difficulty they can refer to the wall to help them solve the new word.

- *Sight words*—Struggling readers require focused instruction and repetition that uses multi-sensory strategies and materials.

  EXAMPLE: A student who is having difficulty with sight words often benefits from having the word written on a card in crayon. The student then traces the word several times. When the student thinks he or she knows the word, the student turns the card over and writes the word in pencil. He or she then self-checks. Each student can have his or her own stack of cards.

- *Vocabulary development*—often the area of greatest deficit. Vocabulary instruction must be relevant to the students and must include multiple exposures to each new word. Also, it is critical that the most important words receive the most attention.

  TIP: On average, students will need to use a word 8-15 times in a meaningful context before it becomes part of their repertoire. It is helpful if struggling students have opportunities to use the word in many different ways—illustrating the word, explaining the word to another person, listening for the word, linking the word to related words, categorizing the word, dramatizing the word, or using the word in their writing.

C. **Syntax Instruction**—Struggling readers often have difficulty predicting words because of a lack of understanding of the structure of written language. This is a particularly difficult skill for ESL/ELL students. Struggling readers need specific instruction on unusual language patterns.

TIP: With simple sentences, students benefit from predicting a missing word in the sentence. When sentences are complex, it is helpful if the text is read aloud or tape recorded so that the student can hear the language. Any identified area of concern can become a mini-lesson focusing on that particular skill.

D. **Comprehension Instruction**—If struggling readers have been told "to sound it out" as their primary strategy, they may not see comprehension as the goal of reading. Struggling readers must be asked over and over, "Does it make sense?" The instructional focus of read aloud, shared reading, and guided reading must be on comprehension. Pre-reading strategies are critical for struggling readers.

> TIP: Struggling readers often benefit from visual information, so providing a picture, illustration, chart, or drawing prior to reading improves comprehension. The pre-reading discussion also allows the teacher to clarify any misconceptions that the student might have and to set a purpose for the reading that will clarify the information.

E. **Read Aloud**—Modeling with high interest materials is critical for struggling students, ideally 4-7 times per day. Read aloud increases students' interest in reading and provides the teacher with multiple opportunities for instruction specifically aimed at struggling readers.

> EXAMPLE: Books with an emotional hook, such as *Where the Red Fern Grows* (1984) by Rawls, or humorous topics, such as *The Twits* (1998) by Dahl, can entice the struggling reader.

F. **Shared Reading**—Struggling readers can experience success through shared reading. It helps them gain a sense of story, understand the concepts of print, and participate in fluent reading.

> TIP: With older students, transparencies on the overhead projector work well for shared reading. This is a great way to increase fluency and focus on language structure.

G. **Guided Reading**—Struggling readers must be reading in instructional-level fiction and nonfiction materials. The lessons need to be designed to meet their unique needs, provide teacher modeling, and create multiple opportunities for rereading to achieve fluency.

- *Pre-Reading strategies* will engage struggling students by generating interest, establishing purpose, providing background knowledge, making connections, encouraging higher-level thinking, predicting content, and developing essential vocabulary. The specific strategy should be selected based on the needs of the struggling reader.

  > TIP: When struggling readers lack background knowledge, the teacher can link new topics to the students' prior knowledge; this leads to increased reading success.

  > EXAMPLE: Struggling readers did not have the essential vocabulary. Prior to reading the teacher selected those words the students needed to experience success and used activities that would connect these words to the students' lives.

- *During-Reading strategies* will help struggling readers monitor their reading, maintain focus, confirm their predictions, and reinforce vocabulary.

  TIP: When students have difficulty staying focused during the reading, the text can be chunked into short sections with specific questions for each section. This helps students stay focused and helps them locate critical information.

  TIP: If struggling readers have difficulty visualizing images, they can benefit from the idea of a VCR or movie in their heads—as they read, they can pause, stop, rewind, and fast forward as necessary to comprehend what they are reading. This idea needs to be modeled, but it can encourage struggling readers to reread.

- *After-Reading strategies* should promote comprehension by helping struggling readers extend what was read by questioning the content, connecting to the content, and responding to what they have read.

  EXAMPLE: When struggling readers were reading the words but not connecting to the text, the teacher had students discuss how the material related to their own lives. This helped these students to develop a deeper understanding of the text.

H. **Literacy Centers**—Centers can provide meaningful practice opportunities if the activities focus on the skills taught during guided reading, are on students' instructional levels, and students are held accountable. Struggling readers need more practice and repetition—literacy centers can provide these opportunities. However, struggling readers often have difficulty staying focused on what they are doing because reading and writing are difficult. Therefore, it is critical that procedures be put in place to hold students accountable for their literacy center work.

  TIP: Students can have a two-pocket folder where they keep their literacy center work. These folders can be turned in as often as necessary to provide teacher monitoring. Struggling students need to demonstrate what they did while at the center. This can be as simple as recording the words they read, describing what they read, or listing the activities they completed.

I. **Literature Circles**—Often struggling readers have never read an entire book. It is critical that books be on their instructional level, but struggling readers can learn to love reading by participating in literature circles.

  EXAMPLE: Select literature circle books around a theme, but at many different reading levels. Struggling readers can participate in discussions around the theme, but read on their instructional levels. Also, nonfiction articles and books are often of greater interest to the struggling reader.

J. **Independent Reading**—Struggling readers must have opportunities to read in materials at their independent reading level. Students reading at the 90th percentile read 40 minutes per day while students reading at the 10th percentile read 1.6 minutes per day (Anderson, Wilson, & Fielding, 1988). Struggling readers do not select to read because reading is difficult. Therefore, it is critical that struggling readers experience success.

  TIP: Read aloud the first chapter of many different books to set the scenes of the books and to entice students to read.

K. **Opportunities to Build Fluency**—Struggling readers must have opportunities for meaningful repetition. Fluency strengthens comprehension.

> TIP: Students benefit from having phrases underlined or highlighted so that they can read the phrase rather than read word by word.

> TIP: It is important that struggling readers learn to self-correct. Often they wait for the teacher to provide feedback. This reduces fluency.

> TIP: One highly successful strategy is to tape stories and content area materials for students. They can listen to a fluent reader, matching the text to the tape.

L. **Using Visuals**—Struggling readers often focus on unimportant details and miss the critical information. Graphic organizers can help students organize information, provide structure, and keep students focused on what they are reading. A graphic organizer identifying the main idea and supporting details is particularly effective with struggling readers.

> TIP: Whenever possible provide visual information, including pictures, photos, colored transparencies, real-life materials, and drawings.

M. **Writing to Support Reading**—Many struggling readers learn to read through writing.

- *Modeled writing* can provide opportunities for teachers to focus on the specific identified needs of struggling readers including sense of story, concepts of print, phonics, vocabulary, or language structure.

- *Interactive writing* encourages struggling students to share the pen and reinforces skills taught in modeled writing. It is critical that struggling students experience success. The students should not be given the pen unless the teacher is confident of a successful experience.

  > TIP: Teachers may do interactive writing activities during small group guided reading instruction or meet with a student prior to interactive writing to ensure success.

- *Pattern writing* increases success by allowing the struggling reader to build on known patterns.

  > EXAMPLE: Provide literature examples, such as *The Important Book* (1990) by Brown, and allow students to use the model provided. As they gain confidence, they will begin to risk and to write their own stories. Also, it helps if students are provided with a word bank of words they might want to include in their writing.

- *Structured writing* provides explicit writing instruction. This instruction can be custom designed to meet the needs of the struggling reader and can reinforce reading instruction.

  > EXAMPLE: Identifying the main idea is one skill area that was creating problems for struggling readers. Students wrote titles for photos, stories, and newspaper articles. The teacher discovered that if students could write the main idea, they could also identify the main idea when they were reading.

- *Spelling instruction* should be based on students' writing. A limited number of high-utility words should be taught. Then students should be expected to use these words correctly all the time. If struggling students practice words incorrectly, it takes much more time to "unlearn" and "relearn" these words.

    TIP: Limit the number of words being taught but expect them to be used correctly all the time. Select those words the student has the greatest need to know.

SAFETY NET 4

USE OF INSTRUCTIONAL TIME
Instructional time is critical. Is instructional time being effectively maximized?

A. **Classroom time**—All students benefit from 90-120 minutes per day on literacy. Struggling readers need even more time. If struggling readers are receiving extra reading support, it is critical that the instruction coordinate with classroom instruction. Push-in programs where specialists work in the classroom are often more effective than pull-out programs because they are easier to coordinate with the classroom program and students are not removed from their classmates.

B. **Time on task**—Struggling readers need to be on task 90-95% of the time. Struggling readers generally excel at avoiding the task, so teachers must be experts at classroom management to help struggling students stay focused.

    EXAMPLE: Tape a card on each students' desk. Put a tally on the card if the student is on task. Establish goals for an increasing number of tallies.

C. **Teaching the same skill all day long**—Struggling readers benefit from having the same skill presented in different subject areas. This reinforces the initial instruction and helps students see the value of the skill.

    TIP: If main idea and details are taught in reading, they can also be taught simultaneously in social studies and science.

D. **Tutorial time**—Several districts have found success by providing short, focused 10-minute tutorial lessons on specific skills.

E. **Minimizing interruptions**—Instructional time can be maximized if interruptions are reduced.

    TIP: Many schools are limiting intercom announcements and reducing the time students spend going to special services by having the services come to the students.

SAFETY NET 5

APPROPRIATE MATERIALS

Appropriate materials are essential for meeting the needs of the struggling reader. Does the school have adequate materials both in terms of quantity and variety for meeting the needs of struggling readers?

A. **Quantity**—300+ titles are needed for each classroom library. Do classroom libraries have a minimum of 300 books? Are there age-appropriate, high-interest reading materials on struggling readers' independent levels?

B. **Sets of leveled fiction and nonfiction books** should be available for guided reading—In the primary grades approximately 200 titles should be available and in intermediate grades a minimum of 40-50 titles should be available. Many struggling readers prefer nonfiction materials. Do classrooms have enough books for guided reading groups? Are the books on the instructional levels of your struggling students?

C. **Variety of formats**—Struggling readers benefit from a variety of formats, including books, poems, magazines, comics, brochures, bumper stickers, riddles, newspapers, postcards, posters, and recipes. Often struggling readers do not generalize and need specific instruction in each of these formats. Are many different formats available and being taught?

> TIP: Magazines like *Click, Cricket,* or *Sports Illustrated for Kids* are very successful with struggling readers.

D. **Variety of genres**—The goal is to entice struggling readers by providing a variety of genres including nonfiction, history, mystery, biography, science fiction, fantasy, and realistic fiction. Often struggling readers prefer materials such as magazines, articles, and short, focused books. Are students being taught many different genres?

E. **Print-Rich environment**—Struggling readers can be supported by a print-rich environment. Are word walls, word charts, spelling charts, homonym charts, graphic organizers, and other supportive materials being used?

F. **School libraries**—High-success schools have libraries that are open and available with many appropriate reading materials (60,000 books available; Krashen, 1993) while poverty schools have limited libraries (20,000 or fewer; Krashen, 1993). How many books are available in your library? How many of these books are appropriate for struggling readers? How many books can students check out at any one time? Is your library accessible to students? Is your librarian able to guide struggling readers in book selection?

G. **Multimedia**—Struggling readers benefit from having frustration-level books recorded on audio tapes or VCR tapes. Are Books-On-Tape and VCR recordings readily available for struggling students?

> TIP: Recorded books can be purchased from www.recordedbooks.com

H. **Computer software**—Great software is available for struggling readers. It can be motivational as well as educational.

- The best programs include sound where students can ask to have words read to them and the computer keeps track of the requested words. This allows the teacher to provide follow-up instruction.

- Word processing with a spell checker and grammar checker helps the struggling reader and writer by highlighting questionable spelling and grammar.

- Creative resources for meeting specific, unusual needs can be found in the field of assistive technology.

  TIP: One good resource is Closing the Gap— www.closingthegap.com

  CONSIDERATION: The computer does not replace the teacher; it has been proven that computers can be motivational, but struggling readers benefit more from a teacher.

I. **Manipulatives**—Multi-sensory options are important for reinforcing reading and word study. Yet, it is also critical that these activities transfer to reading. Words for study should be taken from students' reading. Some options include the following:

- *Alphabet manipulatives*—foam, tiles, cards, magnetic, magnetic foam, wheels, letter cubes, picture tiles, dice, tactile cards, twister, and mini-books.

- *Phonics activities*—onset and rime cards, word tiles, and word families activities.

- *Vocabulary activities*—word cards, illustrations of words, compound word puzzles, synonyms puzzles, and magnetic letters for word building.

- *Chalk boards/dry erasable boards.*

Are many different manipulatives available and being used to reinforce struggling students' reading? Are the activities strengthening reading and writing?

J. **Teacher Supplies**—Teachers can help struggling readers achieve greater success by using unique materials such as the following:

- *Highlighter tape and erasable highlighter pens* for identifying words or phrases.

- *Correction or "boo-boo" tape* that can be placed over incorrectly written words.

- *Sentence strips and pocket charts* for sequencing and matching activities.

- *Magnetic tape and magnetic paper* for creating manipulative activities.

- *Chart paper* for modeled and interactive writing.

Do teachers have the supplies that help them meet the needs of struggling readers?

SAFETY NET 6

PROGRAM OPTIONS

Program options can provide additional support for struggling readers, but they must be coordinated with classroom instruction. Have all available options been considered?

A. Some of the **program options** that might be considered include the following: Title I, Special Education, state-funded programs, Reading Recovery, Reading Recovery Adapted (using Reading Recovery strategies with small groups or older students), library programs, looping, and multiage.

B. If a student is participating in any supplemental programs, **coordination between teachers** is essential. Too often struggling readers receive two different types of instruction using different materials which leads to greater confusion rather than enhanced performance.

C. Many large schools are adopting a model of "**schools within a school**." This breaks a large school into smaller units. Students stay within this unit for several years. The advantages are that teachers get to know the students within their school and students experience a stronger sense of belonging. This model has been particularly effective with struggling readers.

D. **All-day kindergarten** has been effective in providing struggling students with additional instructional time.

Research About Retention

Retention is not a successful solution. Research (Shepard and Smith, 1989) has shown the following:

1. Retention has no benefits for either school achievement or personal adjustment.

2. Retention is strongly correlated to later dropping out of school.

3. Two years in kindergarten, even when one year is labeled "transition program," fail to enhance achievement or solve the problem of inadequate school readiness.

4. From the students' perspective retention is negative and hurtful.

SAFETY NET 7

EFFECTIVE USE OF RESOURCES

Resources can be creatively used to maximize their effectiveness. Are there ways to more effectively utilize existing resources? A key to meeting the needs of struggling readers and writers is finding more time for instruction. Some of the following are possible options:

A. Extending Instructional Time

- *Early start/late stay*—Some schools are having one-half of the students come early or stay late to provide more instructional time with a smaller class size.

- *Block schedules*—Some schools are using block schedules as one way of reducing class size during reading and writing instruction.

- *Added-school programs*—These include before, after, evening, or Saturday classes. These can be provided by school staff, mentors, student teachers, community service agencies, etcetera.

- *Summer school programs*—Many schools are providing additional instruction during the summer to reduce the loss typically seen over the summer. This can be tied to teacher training opportunities.

- *Jump start*—Many schools are having struggling students return to school one to two weeks before other students return.

- *After-lunch bunch*—Struggling students meet for fun reading and writing activities after lunch.

- *Once-a-week checkups*—These have been effectively used to monitor students who are demonstrating success, but are not ready to be "turned loose." Checkups have been particularly effective with students leaving Title I or Reading Recovery.

- *Extended day*—Schools with many struggling students have extended the school day.

- *Extended year*—A U.S. school year is typically 180 days. Many other countries have school years of 220 or more days. So, one way of meeting the needs of struggling students is to lengthen the school year.

- *Homework clubs*—In many schools students can receive help with their homework. There are many options, including computer assistance, community libraries, mentors, before-school clubs, after-school clubs, and parent support groups.

B. Effectively Utilizing Existing Personnel

- *Co-teaching* pairs a regular education teacher and a specialist to work with particular classrooms during reading or writing instruction.

- *Reading Specialists* can serve in multiple roles, including providing staff development, teaching struggling students, selecting materials, and making program recommendations.

    TIP: It is critical that the talents of the reading specialists are maximized and that the majority of their time is spent working with students and staff. If their time is taken up with assessment and paper work, then this is an area that should be reviewed.

- *Communication Disorder Specialists* can work with students and staff, often in the classroom. Communication disorder specialists have terrific ideas for language development and communication skills. Their talents are often underutilized.

- *Bilingual Teachers and/or English as Second Language/English Language Learner Teachers* serve bilingual and ESL/ELL students but can also provide language/vocabulary ideas for working with other struggling readers and writers.

- *Social Workers* can provide knowledge of families and involve families in school/learning activities.
- *Librarians* can share knowledge of children's books, order books for struggling readers, and entice students to read.
- *Counselors* may be able to provide classroom assistance, particularly in the areas of self-esteem, behavior issues, and students' time management.
- *Psychologists* can provide relevant assessment data that can help in planning programs for struggling students.
- *Paraprofessionals* may be utilized for limited supplemental instruction if closely supervised and trained. But it is critical to remember that struggling students deserve the very best instruction provided by the most trained staff members.
- *Administrators* can set the expectations for the staff, model outstanding instructional strategies, and make struggling readers and writers a high priority.

C. Other Resource People

Often there are other people who can provide additional supplemental help for struggling students. Some options are as follows:

- *Parent volunteers* may be able to listen to students read or make tapes of books for students.

    TIP: It is particularly valuable to enlist males because so many of the identified struggling readers are boys, and they benefit from seeing and hearing male modeling.

- *Retired citizens* (including retired teachers) can read or write to students and participate in literacy activities.

    TIP: Students can write to nursing home residents. This provides a real reason for writing and builds a connection between generations.

- *Business mentors* may get released time from employers to volunteer at schools, and businesses may subsidize reading programs if the program is specific and focused.

- *Cross-age tutors* or book buddies can be of benefit to both the older student and the younger student.

    EXAMPLE: A school trained the older struggling students in how to coach and prompt their younger book buddies. Each student read with a book buddy once a week for a year. At the end of the year, both the book buddy and the older students showed substantial reading gains. A side benefit was an improvement in attendance for both students.

- *High school students* doing service projects can work with struggling students.

    TIP: Contact the high school counselor to identify potential future teachers and encourage these students to volunteer.

- *Service organizations* may be looking for ways to contribute.

    TIP: Send school goals and needs to the different service organizations with a survey as to how they could help the school meet its goals for struggling readers.

- *College students, including student teachers*, can gain practical experience by volunteering.

    TIP: Some elementary schools request student teachers. Not only can they have an impact on the training these future teachers receive, but the student teachers are also extra resource people.

D. Financial Resources

Finding adequate economic resources can be challenging. Yet there are innovative ways of finding additional funding.

- *Staffing* can be evaluated to see if any allocations should or can be changed.

    EXAMPLE: Some positions might be able to be funded from many different funding sources which allows these people to work with a greater variety of students—special education, Reading Recovery, Title I, and so on.

- *Money spent on supplies and resources* can be reviewed to see if the budget reflects the goals of the building in meeting the needs of struggling students.

- A good source for locating many *different grants* is the Public Education Network Weekly News Blast http://www.publiceducation.org/

SAFETY NET 8

SCHOOLWIDE COMMUNICATION

Schoolwide communication is critical regarding struggling students. Are there good data collection and good communication regarding struggling readers?

A. Do staff members have extensive knowledge of individual struggling readers? Are they using a wide variety of data?

    TIP: More information makes it easier to plan instruction—anecdotal records, running records, story retellings, rubrics, fluency measures, rate of reading, interest and attitude inventories, attendance information, and review of work samples all provide valuable information.

B. Do staff members have adequate knowledge of the reading performance of struggling students? Are there common problems across the grades? Are struggling students making the desired progress? Are the needs of struggling readers and writers being met?

    TIP: Gathering information about all struggling readers might point out areas that need to be addressed across the grades.

    EXAMPLE: When an elementary school looked at all struggling readers, they discovered that students were having difficulty understanding language structure. Every day teachers selected one sentence from students' reading and focused on the language structure. This led to improved student performance in reading and writing.

C. Are there processes in place for discussing struggling readers and writers?

> TIP: There are many different ways to provide discussions. It is critical that some formal structures be in place and that all staff are aware of the processes. Some options include multidisciplinary teams, grade-level teams, and staff meetings.

SAFETY NET 9

FAMILY PROGRAMS

Family programs can creatively involve the families of struggling readers. Are families effectively involved in their child's education?

A. Is parent training available and effective? Are parents trained in strategies such as paired reading and read aloud? Is there an adult education program that improves parenting skills? Are there English classes for non-English speaking parents?

> EXAMPLE: A video was sent home demonstrating paired reading strategies so that parents could see how to read with their students. The response was very positive.

B. Are there involvement opportunities that focus on reading, including literacy parties, book talks, library story times, and student-led conferences?

> EXAMPLE: Student-led conferences had several positive benefits for struggling students. Parents came to school, students became more responsible for their own learning, and teachers had a chance to meet with parents.

C. Are there innovative ways of supporting struggling readers at home—tapes (both audio and video), reading kits, writing kits, book loan programs, homework clubs, book clubs, and educational games?

D. Are there incentives that encourage parents to attend school functions—food, transportation, child care, translators, convenient times, and a valuing of cultural differences? Is the school a comfortable place for parents? Should meetings be held away from school? Should the meetings be shorter in length? Are the topics of interest to parents?

> EXAMPLE: In one community it was determined that parents desired academic excellence, but would not come to the school for a variety of reasons. A homework club was started in the meeting room of the apartment building. Students and their parents attended.

E. Are there support services for families—clothing, health care, school supplies, book lists, public library information, and access to community services?

F. Are there many different types of communication with the families of struggling readers—good news letters, postcards, success phone calls, and email messages.

> EXAMPLE: A school didn't wait for huge changes but celebrated small steps. These celebrations of success led to more success.

G. Are there new parent programs—welcoming committees, buddies, newcomer kits, student handbooks, and information on services available for struggling students?

H. Are there programs which involve fathers and other men in the lives of your struggling students—videos of men reading to children, photos with men reading and writing, and activities specifically designed for males?

SAFETY NET 10

COMMUNITY PROGRAMS

Community programs can provide additional resources. Are there community resources that could support your struggling readers?

A. Are there additional human resources that have not been utilized—partnerships with businesses, organizations, school alumni, YMCA, boys & girls clubs, high school community service programs, or social and health services?

B. Are there additional financial resources—local businesses, service organizations, PTAs, or donors?

SAFETY NET 11

SUPPORTIVE POLICY DECISIONS

Policy decisions impact struggling readers. Are policy decisions supportive of instruction for struggling readers?

Policy decisions can often undermine the efforts of a school. The following are some areas to review to see if the policy decisions at the school level or district level are supportive of instruction for struggling readers.

A. Is there flexibility in the use of school personnel? Are there options available? How restrictive are the policies?

B. Is there flexibility in how time can be used? Can schedules be changed? How much influence does the transportation department have on schedules?

C. Do curriculum adoptions take the needs of struggling readers into consideration? Do standards focus on growth and progress? Can your struggling readers, with support, meet the standards?

D. Are student policies friendly to struggling students? Are there many different options for meeting the needs of struggling readers? Is retention rarely used? Are there attendance incentives?

E. Is there adequate training for staff members in meeting the needs of struggling readers? Are materials available?

F. Is the attitude reflective of the fact that all students are all staff members' responsibility? Is there trust among staff members and administration? Is there mutual respect among all participants—staff, students, and parents?

G. Is there a climate that promotes change and risk taking? Is there an ongoing focus on the needs of struggling students that goes beyond standardized tests or public reporting? Does district leadership understand the needs of struggling readers? Are "home grown" options encouraged?

H. Is there funding available for programs for struggling readers and writers? Are grants and other funding sources encouraged?

I. Is there leadership that expects struggling students to succeed and provides whatever is necessary to ensure that they can succeed?

J. Is reading research used when policy decisions are made? Are there opportunities for input, comment, and questioning?

Summary

Meeting the needs of struggling readers is an ongoing challenge. There are schools with very limited resources that are being very successful. And there are schools with incredible resources that are not being successful. Each school needs to assess what it is doing that is working, what it is doing that is not working, and what it can do to make a difference. There are many different options—each school must choose what works best for their students and their setting, recognizing that a "home grown" program will be the best choice. It is critical that the performance of struggling readers and writers be continually monitored, and the programs continually be reassessed. With a concerted effort struggling readers and writers can achieve success.

Checklist for Meeting the Needs of Struggling Readers

Rate each item on a 1-4 scale.	Low			High
1. Staff members feel supported and trained in meeting the needs of struggling readers.	1	2	3	4
2. Classroom instruction is on struggling readers' instructional levels.	1	2	3	4
3. Instructional time is maximized.	1	2	3	4
4. Appropriate materials are available for struggling readers.	1	2	3	4
5. Multiple program options are available and utilized.	1	2	3	4
6. Retention is rarely used.	1	2	3	4
7. Innovative ways have been found to expand instructional time.	1	2	3	4
8. Personnel are used effectively and creatively to meet the needs of struggling readers.	1	2	3	4
9. Extra funding is consistently being sought.	1	2	3	4
10. Training needs have been identified, and staff training is being provided.	1	2	3	4
11. Communication regarding struggling readers is excellent.	1	2	3	4
12. Families are involved in their children's education.	1	2	3	4
13. Community programs are supportive of the educational needs of struggling readers.	1	2	3	4
14. Policy decisions take into consideration the needs of struggling readers and writers.	1	2	3	4
15. The needs of struggling readers are continually reassessed.	1	2	3	4
16. All staff assume responsibility for all students.	1	2	3	4

SCORING: Any area scoring below a 3 needs further review.

Copyright © 2004 by Corwin Press. All rights reserved. Reprinted from *The Book of Reading and Writing Ideas, Tips, and Lists for the Elementary Classroom* by Sandra E. Anderson. Thousand Oaks, CA: Corwin Press, www.corwinpress.com. Reproduction authorized only for the local school site that has purchased this book.

Chapter 8
Information Gathering
and Data Collection

Success Story

Some Reading Recovery students were making great gains and others were not. Staff members felt the wrong students were receiving Reading Recovery. However, when the school gathered information and data about these students, it was discovered that the students not showing gains were absent on the average of one day per week. Parents were contacted and attendance was stressed. As attendance improved so did reading performance.

Information gathering and data collection are critical when making decisions regarding literacy instruction. Too often changes are made without taking into consideration all of the information and data that might be helpful. The schools and classrooms that are showing the greatest success in strengthening students' literacy performance are consistently looking at all pertinent data. There are no simple answers to complex educational issues, and in order to make the best possible decisions regarding literacy instruction, it is important to collect and utilize data regarding individual students, groups of students, curriculum, instruction, and materials.

STUDENT INFORMATION

1. Are students successful with word study skills—decoding, sight words, vocabulary?
2. Do students comprehend what they are reading?
3. Are students fluent?
4. Can students effectively communicate their ideas in writing?
5. Are students engaged in learning?
6. Do students have self-management skills—ability to organize efficiently and stay on task?

(Continued)

STUDENT INFORMATION (Continued)

7. Do students have test-taking skills?

8. Are students making excellent progress?

9. For those who are not making excellent progress, what interventions have been tried and how successful have they been?

STUDENT SURVEYS OR INTERVIEWS

1. What are students reading?

2. What are they finding easy about reading and writing?

3. What is difficult about reading and writing?

4. What do students think could make reading and writing more interesting? Easier?

5. How do students think they are doing in reading and writing?

GROUP INFORMATION

1. What can be learned by analyzing retention information?

2. Are there ethnic differences in performance?

3. Are there gender differences in performance?

4. How does the performance of English as a Second Language/English Language Learners compare to general education students?

5. How does the performance of special education students compare to general education students?

6. How does the performance of new students compare to students who have been at the school for many years?

7. How does the performance of high mobility students compare to students with low mobility rates?

8. Is there a difference in the performance of students with a high number of discipline referrals compared to those with low discipline referrals?

9. How does the performance of students with high numbers of absences compare to those with a low number of absences?

CURRICULUM AND INSTRUCTION INFORMATION

1. Are all of the components of a balanced reading and writing program being taught?
2. Are flexible guided reading groups being used?
3. Are a wide variety of instructional strategies being used?

MATERIALS INFORMATION

1. Do students have a wide variety of texts available?
2. Are there materials at different reading levels—both for the struggling reader and the high-achieving reader?
3. Are there fiction and nonfiction materials available?

Summary

By collecting and evaluating the data, teachers can make instructional decisions that will best meet students' needs. Data collection may lead to school-wide changes, may identify staff training needs, may impact curriculum and instruction decisions, or may influence material-purchasing decisions. Data collection should be an ongoing part of any literacy program. The schools showing the greatest improvement are effectively utilizing data as they make literacy decisions.

Chapter 9
Staff Training Ideas

One of the greatest challenges is finding time for staff training. By creatively using existing time and innovative strategies, staff training can be maximized.

GROUP PROCESS FOR STAFF TRAINING

1. **Remember When**—Adults are asked to remember when they were in school and how they felt, both positively and negatively. This works well for introducing new topics. Staff members can remember favorite or least favorite teachers, favorite or least favorite subjects, or any other relevant topic.

    EXAMPLE: Staff members were asked to jot down their favorite memories about reading. They then discussed their positive and negative memories. A list was developed and posted in the staff room. Many staff members asked students their favorite memories. The end result was staff members changing some of their classroom practices.

2. **Chalk Talk**—A question is posed on butcher paper. Participants silently write their comments or questions on the butcher paper. This is an effective way of getting initial concerns out on the table. It also provides a way for all participants to voice their concerns. Participants can add on to others' ideas and write questions next to others' ideas. No ideas can be removed.

    EXAMPLE: An elementary staff addressed the question, "How can we best meet the needs of struggling readers?" The suggestions were clustered and considered. This led to many innovative interventions for meeting the needs of struggling readers.

3. **Brainstorming**—This is a way of getting many ideas out on the table. It often works best if a facilitator goes around the room asking each person to provide a response, even if the response is to pass. This encourages participation by all.

    EXAMPLE: A question was posed to the staff—"What are we doing to meet the needs of high-achieving students and what could we do to better meet their needs?" The first meeting generated a list of ideas. At the second meeting, teachers discussed viable options and decided which options should be pursued.

4. **Jigsaw**—The staff is divided into small groups with approximately five people in each group. Each member of the group becomes an expert on a particular topic and then shares this information with the other members of the group.

EXAMPLE: Staff members were formed into groups of five. One member from each group joined others to read an article on a particular pre-reading strategy. The other members of the original group were reading other articles. The expert on this article returned to his or her group and taught the information to the group. This is particularly effective when learning new ideas or strategies.

5. **Butcher Paper Dialogue**—Butcher paper or chart paper is put up in a staff room or other prominent place. A question or area of focus may be identified and then over time participants add comments and create an ongoing dialogue on the topic. This strategy can also be used for feedback on something new that is being tried.

    EXAMPLE: Teachers listed vocabulary instructional strategies they had tried that had been effective. Other teachers added comments and tried some of the new vocabulary strategies.

6. **Study Groups**—Small groups read a particular book, meet to discuss the book, and decide how they can apply what is being learned. The whole group may read the same book, but some of the discussions may take place in smaller groups, giving each person more opportunities to participate.

    TIP: Teachers are more willing to participate if the book is provided for them.

    EXAMPLE: An elementary school selected a book on comprehension strategies. This book was the focus for the entire year. As they read about the different strategies, they experimented in their classrooms and reported on successes or challenges.

7. **Modeling of Strategies**—Instructional strategies are modeled during meetings.

    EXAMPLE: Pre-reading strategies were modeled during a staff meeting as a way of assessing teachers' background knowledge in student assessment. What did the staff know about rubrics, performance-based assessments, writing assessments, running records, and anecdotal records? This led to staff training decisions and encouraged staff members to use this strategy in their classrooms.

8. **Threaded Discussion**—A question or concern is posted to all participants. Individuals respond, with others adding on to the discussion. This works well as an email dialogue where the question starts with one person and his or her response is forwarded on to others.

    EXAMPLE: One question was, "How often are you changing your flexible groups and what information are you using to make the decision?" This led to more sharing and collaboration.

9. **Video Discussion Groups**—An educational video is shown and participants then discuss how the concepts can be applied in classrooms across the grades.

    EXAMPLE: A video was shown on word walls. Staff members then discussed how word walls could be used with their students.

10. **Online Courses**—Individual teachers can be registered for online courses. It is important to provide opportunities for teachers to discuss what they have learned with other teachers.

EXAMPLE: Several staff members took an online course on literacy centers. In addition, they met once a week to plan the implementation of literacy centers.

11. **Carousel**—Several pieces of butcher paper have different topics listed on them. The pieces rotate to different groups. Participants add their comments to the previous comments. Discussions focus on the comments.

     EXAMPLE: This idea was used to identify read alouds for each grade level. One piece of paper was created for each grade level. Staff members listed the read alouds perfect for Grade 1, 2, etcetera. As the sheets rotated, other staff members added titles, questioned titles, or made a note that they wanted a particular title reserved for a specific grade level. This led to more discussions on children's books and the development of a schoolwide read aloud list.

12. **Fishbowl**—A small group models a strategy or has a discussion in the center of the room while the remaining members of the group observe. At the end, members on the outside can contribute comments and/or questions.

     EXAMPLE: A small group reviewed student work samples to see if what they received was what they intended—did the results match the goal or objective? The other members of the staff observed the process and at the end contributed comments and questions. Following this process, grade-level teams more effectively reviewed student work samples to see if their lesson objectives were being achieved.

13. **Sort and Categorize**—Ideas or concerns are listed on 4 x 6 cards. Then the cards are put up on a board where they are sorted and categorized. This helps to identify major ideas or concerns.

     EXAMPLE: Staff members listed supplemental reading materials they thought would be valuable. These were categorized and prioritized. Future purchases were based on this list.

14. **Being an Expert**—Participants are assigned different roles and must critique or analyze the situation from that particular point of view. The different viewpoints are shared. This is helpful when starting a new program that needs to be understood by many different groups. Also, it works well when there is potential conflict and a compromise position may be necessary.

     EXAMPLE: Assessments were viewed from the viewpoints of staff members, district administrators, parents, students, the media, and legislators.

15. **Action Research**—Teachers decide on one or more strategies to implement in their classroom. They collect before and after data to determine how the change has impacted learning.

     EXAMPLE: Staff members collected data on word choice in writing. They then provided mini-lessons on word choice over a one-month period, and re-evaluated students' performance. They were pleased with the improved results.

16. **Triads**—Individuals are clustered into groups of three for discussions and observations. Groups of three work better than partners because the triad tends to provide more balanced discussions. For this strategy to work most effectively, it is important that there is a climate of trust and mutual respect.

EXAMPLE: Primary staff members were working on shared reading. Triads were created and each member of the triad was observed by the other two members of their triad during a shared reading lesson. They then met to discuss the shared reading lessons. Staff members learned from each other.

17. **Book Talks**—Individual teachers do a book talk about a book they have read. This can be a children's book, an adult book, or an educational book.

EXAMPLE: One teacher did a book talk on a new book of instructional strategies. Other teachers were interested in the book and formed a study group using the book as a focus.

18. **Make-and-Take**—Teachers can meet to create materials to be used in their classroom.

EXAMPLE: Staff members met to create literacy center materials, big books with accompanying materials, and literature circle materials.

19. **Learning Consortiums**—Activities can be planned around learning groups that include educators within a school and from outside the school.

EXAMPLE: A school partnered with a university to study time on task. The college provided the research and theory while the staff provided the practical implementation. College students studying education participated in observations and discussions. These meetings became true theory-into-practice learning sessions.

Finding Time for Staff Development

There are many creative ways of finding time for staff development. The following are just a few ideas that other schools have found to be effective:

- **Staff meetings**—The day-to-day informational items are handled in writing and staff meetings are used for staff development. If announcements are at the end of the staff meeting, they are shorter and more focused.

- **Grade-level meetings**—To maintain focus, it is often helpful to set up reporting procedures for what was discussed.

- **Lunch bunches**—More effective discussions seem to occur if lunch is provided.

- **Before-school/after-school study groups**—If a book is provided and the activity is voluntary, participation will increase.

- **Cross-grade level partnering**—A primary and an intermediate teacher become partners. One teacher takes both classes for an activity. They rotate so that each teacher has time to learn new strategies or to plan the implementation of new instructional procedures. Teachers benefit from the extra time, students benefit from the cross-age activities.

- **Substitutes teaching a variety of classes**—Substitutes can rotate through different grades teaching each grade for one hour. Generic classroom activities can be planned so that teachers do not have extra planning. This works well for grade-level planning around new ideas or changes.

- **Mentors**—A mentor can work with another staff member. Mentors are particularly effective with staff members new to a school.
- **Planning times**—Many schools provide common planning times for grade-level teams.

Staff training is the key to bringing about change. Creative and innovative ways can be found to provide staff training.

Chapter 10
Fifty 10-Minute Tips for "Leaders" to Use to Impact the Reading and Writing Performance of Students

The following is a list of ideas that can be used by principals, reading specialists, teachers, or other school leaders to positively influence the school's literacy program. A principal could give this list to a superintendent. A teacher could provide the principal with a copy of the ideas. An entire staff could decide which of these ideas they would like to implement. Schools that make a concerted effort to focus on literacy demonstrate the greatest gains.

1. Drop by a class with your favorite book and read to students for 10 minutes. This could be a complete picture book or a chapter or two of a longer book. If reading a chapter, then leave the book for the teacher to finish reading at a future date.

2. Ask a teacher to invite you to be a guest reader for one day.

3. Have students at many different grade levels send you their favorite read aloud titles. Post the titles in your office, the hall, the Board Room, or publish in a newsletter.

4. Ask parents to send their titles of favorite read aloud books. Post the list or send the list to students.

5. Tape record a favorite book and send tapes to classrooms for listening times. It is helpful if the book that was used can be sent with the tape. You can use an office call dinger to indicate the turning of the pages.

6. Read a short, humorous piece, such as a poem, over the intercom.

7. Invite bus drivers, cooks, and community members to be guest readers or to talk about how they use reading and writing in their jobs.

8. Put a favorite poem on an overhead transparency and take it to a classroom to share. Leave the transparency for students to use.

9. Have students create class big books for your room or office.

10. Collect favorite shared reading titles and share with other schools; for example, The Favorite Big Books from Room 12 at ___Elementary School.

11. Drop in for a guided reading lesson and observe the lesson or introduce the new book to students by establishing their prior knowledge about the topic.

12. Use a pre-reading strategy for one of your staff meetings. For example, use an anticipation guide as an introduction to a topic.

13. Observe a Title I, Reading Recovery, or Special Education reading lesson.

14. Have students send you an after-reading activity showing how they connected to the text. Respond to the class, telling how you would relate to the text.

15. Have students send you a new word or phrase and how it was used in context, including an illustration of the word. Post the vocabulary words in your office or put these words in a newsletter.

16. Have students send you lists of their favorite books, write book reviews, and make recommendations for future book purchases.

17. Ask students to research and recommend books on social studies or science topics that would be good additions to a school collection.

18. Notify students of a book you are reading, why you selected this particular book, and how you will evaluate it.

19. Have students design, create, and send you book jackets for favorite books. Post book jackets in a prominent place in the school, district, or public library.

20. Visit a class and write a real-life memo on the overhead as a model for students.

21. Send an email to several classrooms as an example of a message you might write. Have students edit and return the email or have students submit questions they have regarding the email.

22. Visit a classroom and participate in interactive writing by having students share the pen with you.

23. Send students an interesting piece of writing—descriptive, expository, or persuasive— and tell them why you found this piece to be particularly interesting.

24. Have different classrooms send you a favorite piece of writing from one of the students. Put together a collection of favorite grade-level writings to share with others.

25. Have students send you great openers or beginnings that they think you could use.

26. Have students write the multiple-choice questions to accompany a standardized reading passage and then send the sample questions to you. Provide feedback on the quality of the questions.

27. Have students write a series of writing prompts that they think should be used for school, district, or state assessments. Have them justify why these are good writing prompts. Respond to their ideas.

28. Have students send you a list of nonfiction topics the class has brainstormed as high-interest writing topics.

29. Share something you have written with students and teachers.

30. Visit a classroom and read a tongue twister book like *Timid Timothy's Tongue Twisters* (1986) by Gackenbach.

31. Send a favorite alphabet book to primary classrooms for their enjoyment.

32. Have students send you their illustrated alphabet books and put these books on display.

33. Send students via email a word of the week. Have students illustrate the word or guess why you selected this word.

34. Send a new content area word to an appropriate grade level. Have students determine the significance of this particular word.

35. Visit a classroom and have students explain new words that they have recently learned.

36. Send students a sentence or two and have them expand the sentences to include more descriptive words.

37. Send students several short sentences and have them combine or rewrite the sentences.

38. Send students a sentence with a word or two left out to see if they can guess the missing word.

39. Send students an interesting article from a newspaper minus the title and have them write the headline.

40. Send students a topic of study and have them return to you what they already know about the topic and what they would like to learn about the topic.

41. Visit a classroom and ask several students what they are reading, why they are reading this particular material, and what they find interesting or how it relates to their own lives.

42. Have students write what they like best about their teacher, the school, or the district. Students can also write about favorite school memories.

43. Have students time their transition times, wasted time, or time off task and report their results. Ask them to set reasonable goals for improvement and obtain follow-up data.

44. Collect innovative ideas for involving parents in the school reading and writing program. Publish ideas in parent newsletters.

45. Photocopy school or district goals on large paper and have students explain the goals. Create business cards with school or district goals to send to parents and staff.

46. Collect ideas from students on what makes an effective school and an effective literacy program.

47. Collect favorite titles from different grades by genre. Then publish the lists.

48. Send out a strategy of the week and ask staff members to let you know how they used the strategy.

49. Subscribe to a reading or writing journal and share articles with staff members.

50. Have fun with reading and writing and let others know.

Chapter 11
101 Parent Tips to Enhance Literacy

Each of these ideas can be adapted to different ages of students by varying the degree of difficulty or utilizing more or less challenging materials.

1. Send parents a recommended read-aloud list by grade level, encouraging parents to read materials above their students' instructional levels.

2. Send parents a list of books that have been read aloud in the classroom so they can read them again with their students or discuss them at home.

3. Send audiotapes with books to be read aloud at home.

4. Send videotapes that model reading aloud. You can also send the book so that students and parents can read along with the videotape.

5. Have volunteers tape record content area material and send the tape and content area text home.

6. Send home a word of the week with suggestions for using the word, finding the word, illustrating the word, and writing the word.

7. Send a small collection of magnetic letters or letter cards and have students make as many words as possible from these letters and record their words.

8. Send sticky notes and have parents label things around the house. This can be more sophisticated by labeling tools, kitchen utensils, and hobby items.

9. Send clip boards and have students write words they find around their home.

10. Send photographs taken in the classroom and have families write the captions to go with the photographs. The same thing can be done with magazine photos or newspaper photos.

11. Have families send a photo they have taken with a caption. These make great bulletin boards.

12. Send home a news article and have families write the headline or title.

13. Have students, with the help of their families, write directions for something they have done at home. It is helpful to send a sample.

14. Create bookbags for sending home books. Include the following in the bookbag: books, questions to discuss, activities to do, and paper for illustrating what happened in the book.

15. Have parents write notes to place in student's lunches or backpacks.

16. Provide parents with a list of children's magazines.

17. Send a stuffed animal and have families write about the adventures of the animal. Include writing paper, illustration paper, and different kinds of writing implements. This can rotate among homes with new chapters for each home.

18. Send home dry erasable boards and pens for word practice.

19. Send home puppets for storytelling. An inexpensive way of doing this is to use paper bag puppets.

20. Send a tape of sounds and see if families can identify the sounds.

21. Send several sentences with a few words missing. Have families brainstorm what words could fit in the missing blanks.

22. Cut the text and illustrations apart and send home for families to match the text to the illustrations.

23. Send a set of vocabulary words and have families guess what topic or theme is being studied.

24. Create a spreadsheet with different columns for 2-syllable words, 3-syllable words, 4-syllable words, and 5-syllable words. Have families brainstorm or find words to fit in each category. This same activity can be done with many different skills—words beginning with a particular letter, ending with a particular letter, etcetera.

25. Cut up a cartoon strip and have families sequence the cartoon strip. These can be cartoons created by the students.

26. Have students draw a cartoon character and take the character home. Ask families to add the speaking and thinking bubbles.

27. Have students illustrate vocabulary words and then take the illustrations home to see if their families can match the words to the illustrations.

28. Send home riddles or jokes. Have families collect new jokes or riddles. Preview for appropriateness. They can also write clues for "What Am I?" or "Who Am I?"

29. Send examples of figurative language and have families illustrate the sayings. It is helpful to send a completed sample as a model.

30. Send a simple story and have families identify the beginning, middle, and end. A graphic organizer can provide structure and organization. This can be made more difficult by increasing the difficulty of the story or text.

31. Send a nonfiction piece and a fiction piece and have families list the facts.

32. Send a nonfiction piece and have families decide what would go in the index that would accompany the text.

33. Have families collect real-life materials to send to school—menus, ads, junk mail, etcetera. These can be effectively utilized in literacy centers.

34. Send a word and have families generate rhyming words, including multisyllabic words.

35. Send strips of adding machine tape and have families write one word for each letter of the alphabet. This can be linked to topics of study such as animals, sea life, or history.

36. Send a list of prepositions and have families illustrate the meanings.

37. Send white inexpensive paper plates and have students with their families illustrate opposites—example fast on one side, slow on the other.

38. Send a list of related words and have families place the words on a continuum—examples include jog, run, stroll, saunter.

39. Send a sample of a content area web and have families add other information to the web. Follow with a new web of a future unit and have families put down what they know about the topic.

40. Send a picture that includes lots of objects and have families label or list the objects.

41. Send a board game home for students to play at home.

42. Have students and families create a new board game with directions. The game may be created around a particular book.

43. Have students and families tape record or video record a favorite family story.

44. Send home magnetic word cards for students to use on the refrigerator—words can be read, alphabetized, grouped by number of syllables, etcetera.

45. Send sentence strips that can be sequenced—they can include the words first, next, last, or finally.

46. Send sentence strips that have been cut up and have students put back together and record their sentence(s).

47. Send humorous books and have families write a list of reasons why the book is funny.

48. Send 20 words and have families select 5 words to use in a paragraph or story.

49. Have families turn off the television for 60 minutes and write all the things they did during the 60 minutes.

50. Have families create word collections—people words, color words, grumpy words, etcetera.

51. Have families collect unusual sounding words—examples bamboozle, gazebo, whoosh.

52. Have students read to a senior citizen or older relative.

53. Have families write synonyms or related words for particular overused words such as nice, run, or said.

54. Have families use a familiar song to write a new version such as "Old MacDonald Had a Zoo."

55. Ask families to send a personal museum for their child—items or memorabilia that have meaning. The number of items can be limited and students can write why each is important.

56. Have parents write endings to the sentence starter—When I was young, . . .

57. Send readers theater plays that can be read at home. Parents can take some parts and children other parts.

58. Ask families to generate character descriptions or all the words they can think of to describe a familiar character—for example, Barney.

59. Send 20 words and have families sort the words into no more than 5 categories and label each category.

60. Send sight word lists that can be posted on the refrigerator. Use a large font and add to or change the list periodically.

61. Have students create flip books where the onset goes on the first segment and the rime on the second. Blank pages can be left for students to add words at home.

62. Have families illustrate homophones after sending home several examples.

63. Send magic slates with word lists for writing practice.

64. Send a table of contents and an index and have families compare the two—how are they alike and how are they different.

65. Send a paragraph from a content area book and have families write the heading for that section.

66. Send a colored photo or illustration on a transparency with overhead pens and have families write the text to accompany the photo or illustration.

67. Send a sample letter and have students write a new letter to a family member.

68. Send one line of a poem home each day (not necessarily in order). Have students create a new poem by placing the sentences in the order of their choice.

69. Send a sample acrostic and have students create an acrostic for each family member.

70. Send a sample alliteration and have families write new alliterations. This can be structured in many different ways—for example, it can be limited to particular letter of the alphabet.

71. Have students collect magazine or newspaper ads and then create a new ad or a new product.

72. Have families create a timeline of their child's life—a sample can be sent as a model.

73. Have families write a book jacket or create a new book cover for a book.

74. Send a list of descriptive words and have students create a character from those words.

75. Have families write the directions from their home to the school.

76. Send a short story without an ending and have families tape record or write story endings.

77. Have families write Good News/Bad News books about a topic—for example, the good news about summer vacation/the bad news about summer vacation.

78. Send examples of greeting cards and have families create their own greeting cards.

79. Have families identify their favorite sentence or favorite words from a particular selection.

80. Send postcards and have families write concise messages—often stores will give schools old postcards.

81. Send surveys or questionnaires and have families complete them at home.

82. Have families collect and send to school sports trivia.

83. Ask families to have conversations around different topics such as "the worst trouble I ever got in," "my proudest moment," or "my most embarrassing moment."

84. Have families create lists of palindromes—words that read the same forwards as backwards—like radar or pup.

85. Have families taste a food item and then write adjectives to describe the food.

86. Send home multiple meaning words and have families identify all the ways the word could be used such as the word "charge."

87. Send home a word that can be used in many different contexts or forms and have families list the different ways it can be used, such as safe, safeguard, safety.

88. Send home a sample of an advice column and have students write a new advice column. This can be effectively used for social issues occurring at school.

89. Send a mystery and have families propose how to solve the mystery—*Encyclopedia Brown* mysteries by Sobol work well as starters.

90. Have students record all household tasks that must be completed for the family to function.

91. Send home a bag with mystery items. Have families predict a story based on the mystery items.

92. Have students make content area word collections—for example, all words relating to math.

93. Send a sample of a tongue twister and have students write new ones.

94. Have families write their daily schedule.

95. Send a variety of schedules and have families locate specific information—for example, airline schedules or bus schedules.

96. Send a fairy tale and have families retell the story from another point of view—*The True Story of the Three Pigs by A. Wolf* by Scieszka is a great model.

97. Have parents send examples of letterheads, business cards, brochures, etcetera.

98. Set up a book exchange where parents can trade books—both adult books and children's books.

99. Invite parents to be guest readers at school.

100. Provide public library card applications for families.

101. Have parents identify their favorite childhood book. Select some titles to read and discuss with students.

Conclusion

Teachers have the greatest impact on students' learning. When evaluating your own classroom, the following are some questions that might be helpful in determining areas of strength and areas that need further focus:

- Do I have a complete, comprehensive literacy program?
- Are all essential reading and writing skills being taught?
- Does my reading instruction enhance my writing instruction?
- Does instruction align to students' needs?
- Is reading instruction on students' instructional levels?
- Do I need more materials or training?

When groups of teachers work together to strengthen literacy, they have even greater impact. Questions you may want to address include:

- Is literacy a school priority?
- Is there alignment across the grades?
- Do we talk about student performance, instruction, successes, and concerns?
- Are there safety nets for struggling students?
- Is there support for literacy instruction?

All students deserve the very best possible reading and writing instruction. With a concerted effort it is possible to create an outstanding reading and writing program where dramatic results are obtained.

References and Suggested Readings

Ada, Alma Flor. (2001). *With Love, Little Red Hen*. New York: Atheneum.

Adams, Marilyn. (1990). *Beginning to Read: Thinking and Learning About Print*. Cambridge, MA: MIT Press.

Allen, Janet. (1999). *Words, Words, Words: Teaching Vocabulary in Grades 4–12*. Portland, ME: Stenhouse.

Allington, Dick, and Cunningham, Patricia. (1999). *Classrooms That Work*. New York: Longman.

Allington, Richard L. (2001). *What Really Matters for Struggling Readers: Designing Research-Based Programs*. New York: Longman.

Allington, Richard L., and Cunningham, Patricia. (2002). *Schools That Work: Where All Children Read and Write*. Boston: Allyn & Bacon.

Anderson, R. C., Wilson, P., and Fielding, L. (1988). Growth in Reading and How Children Spend Their Time Outside of School. *Reading Research Quarterly*, 23(3), 285–303.

Atwell, Nancie. (1998). *In the Middle: New Understandings About Writing, Reading, and Learning*. Portsmouth, NH: Heinemann.

Bayer, Jane, and Steven Kellogg. (1992). *A My Name Is Alice*. New York: Dial.

Beck, Isabel, McKeown, Margaret, Hamilton, Rebecca, and Kucan, Linda. (1997). *Questioning the Author: An Approach for Enhancing Student Engagement With Text*. Newark, DE: International Reading Association.

Billmeyer, Rachel, and Barton, Mary Lee. (1998). *Teaching Reading in the Content Areas: If Not Me, Then Who?* Aurora, CO: Mid-Continent Regional Educational Laboratory.

Bouffler, Chrystine. (Ed.). (1992). *Literacy Evaluation: Issues and Practicalities*. Portsmouth, NH: Heinemann.

Brandreth, Gyles Daubeney, and Alex Chin. (1992). *The Biggest Tongue Twister Book in the World*. New York: Puffin.

Brown, Margaret Wise. (1990). *The Important Book*. New York: Harper Trophy.

Brownlie, Faye, and Close, Susan. (1992). *Beyond Chalk & Talk*. Markham, Ontario: Pembroke.

Buehl, Doug. (2001). *Classroom Strategies for Interactive Learning*. Newark, DE: International Reading Association.

Calkins, Lucy McCormick. (1983). *The Art of Teaching Writing*. Portsmouth, NH: Heinemann.

Calkins, Lucy McCormick. (2001). *The Art of Teaching Reading*. New York: Longman.

Cambourne, Brian, and Turbill, Jan. (Eds.). (1994). *Responsive Evaluation*. Portsmouth, NH: Heinemann.

Clymer, Theodore. (1996). The Utility of Phonic Generalizations in the Primary Grades. *The Reading Teacher*, 50(3), 182–187.

Cooney, Barbara. (1982). *Miss Rumphius*. New York: Puffin.

Cunningham, Patricia. (1995). *Phonics They Use: Words for Reading and Writing*. New York: HarperCollins.

Dahl, Roald. (1998). *The Twits*. New York: Puffin.

Daniels, Harvey. (1994). *Literature Circles: Voices and Choice in the Student-Centered Classroom*. Portland, ME: Stenhouse.

Doolittle, Bev. (2000). *The Earth Is My Mother*. New York: Greenwich Workshop Press.

Dubowski, Mark. (1998). *Ice Mummy: The Discovery of a 5,000-Year-Old Man*. New York: Random House.

Epstein, Joyce. (1995). School/Family/Community Partnerships: Caring for the Children We Share. *Phi Delta Kappan*, 76(9), 701–712.

Epstein, Joyce, Sanders, Mavis G., Simon, Beth, Salinas, Karen Clark, Jansorn, Natalie Rodriguez, and Van Voorhis, Frances L. (2002). *School, Family and Community Partnerships: Your Handbook for Action*. 2nd ed. Thousand Oaks, CA: Corwin.

Erickson, John R. (1998). *The Case of the Swirling Killer Tornado*. New York: Viking Children's Books.

Fisher, Bobbi, and Medvic, Emily Fisher. (2000). *Perspectives on Shared Reading: Planning & Practice*. Portsmouth, NH: Heinemann.

Fitzpatrick, Jo. (1997). *Phonemic Awareness: Playing With Sounds to Strengthen Beginning Reading Skills*. Cypress, CA: Creative Teaching Press.

Fleischman, Sid. (1986). *The Whipping Boy*. New York: Harper Trophy.

Fountas, Irene, and Pinnell, Gay Su. (1996). *Guided Reading: Good First Teaching for All Children*. Portsmouth, NH: Heinemann.

Fountas, Irene, and Pinnell, Gay Su. (1999). *Matching Books to Readers: Using Leveled Books in Guided Reading K–3*. Portsmouth, NH: Heinemann.

Fountas, Irene, and Pinnell, Gay Su. (2001). *Guiding Readers and Writers Grades 3–6*. Portsmouth, NH: Heinemann.

Fullan, Michael. (1993). *Change Forces: Probing the Depths of Educational Reform*. Bristol, PA: Falmer.

Fullan, Michael, and Stiegelbauer, Suzanne. (1991). *The New Meaning of Educational Change*. New York: Teachers College Press.

Gackenbach, Dick. (1986). *Timid Timothy's Tongue Twisters*. New York: Holiday House.

Giorgis, Cyndi, and Pollack, Judy. (1999). Picture Books Containing Examples of Literary Devices. *English Journal*, 88(4), 31–33.

Gregory, Gayle, and Chapman, Carol. (2002). *Differentiated Instructional Strategies: One Size Doesn't Fit All*. Thousand Oaks, CA: Corwin.

Hart, Betty, and Risley, Todd. (1995). *Meaningful Differences in the Everyday Experiences of Young Children*. Baltimore: Brookes.

Hart-Hewins, Linda, Wells, Jan, and Stratton, Philippa. (1999). *Better Books! Better Readers! How to Choose, Use, and Level Books for Children in the Primary Grades*. Portland, ME: Stenhouse.

Harvey, Brett. (1986). *My Prairie Year*. New York: Holiday House.

Harvey, Stephanie. (1998). *Nonfiction Matters: Reading, Writing, and Research in Grades 3–8*. Portland, ME: Stenhouse.

Harvey, Stephanie, and Goudvis, Anne. (2000). *Strategies That Work: Teaching Comprehension to Enhance Understanding*. Portland, ME: Stenhouse.

Heacox, Diane. (2002). *Differentiating Instruction in the Regular Classroom: How to Reach and Teach All Learners, Grades 3–12*. Minneapolis, MN: Free Spirit Publishing.

Heller, Ruth. (1989). *Many Luscious Lollipops: A Book About Adjectives*. New York: Puffin.

Herber, Harold L. (1978). *Teaching Reading in Content Areas*. Englewood Cliffs, NJ: Prentice Hall.

Holcomb, Edie. (1999). *Getting Excited About Data: How to Combine People, Passion, and Proof*. Thousand Oaks, CA: Corwin.

Holdaway, Don. (1979). *Foundations of Literacy*. New York: Scholastic Press.

Holliman, Linda. (1996). *The Complete Guide to Classroom Centers*. Cypress, CA: Creative Teaching Press.

Hooks, William H. (1987). *Moss Gown*. New York: Clarion.

Hord, Shirley, Rutherford, William L., Huling-Austin, Leslie, and Hall, Gene. (1987). *Taking Charge of Change*. Alexandria, VA: Association for Supervision and Curriculum Development.

Hutchins, Pat. (1986). *The Doorbell Rang*. New York: Harper Trophy.

Joffe, Laura. (1985). *If You Give a Mouse a Cookie*. New York: Harper Trophy.

Johnson, Dale, and Pearson, P. David. (1978). *Teaching Reading Vocabulary*. New York: Holt, Rinehart.

Joyce, Bruce. (Ed.). (1990). *Changing School Culture Through Staff Development*. Alexandria, VA: Association for Supervision and Curriculum Development Yearbook.

Joyce, Bruce, and Showers, Beverly. (1995). *Student Achievement Through Staff Development: Fundamentals of School Renewal*. New York: Longman.

Kovacs, Deborah, and Preller, James. (1999). *Meet the Authors and Illustrators: Volumes 1 and 2*. New York: Scholastic Press.

Krashen, Stephen. (1993). *The Power of Reading: Insights From the Research*. Englewood, CO: Libraries Unlimited.

Lane, Barry. (1993). *After the End: Teaching and Learning Creative Revision*. Portsmouth, NH: Heinemann.

Ledbetter, Mary. (1997). *Writing Portfolios Activities Kit*. New York: Prentice Hall.

Lindsay, Thomas. (1986). Effective Reading Programs: Where Is the Principal? *Illinois Reading Council Journal*, 27(4), 16–20.

Lowry, Lois. (1998). *Looking Back: A Book of Memories*. New York: Delacorte.

Markle, Sandra. (1999). *After the Spill: The Exxon Valdez Disaster, Then & Now*. New York: Walker & Co. Library.

Marzano, Robert, Norford, Jennifer, Paynter, Diane, Pickering, Debra J., and Gaddy, Barbara B. (2002). *A Handbook for Classroom Instruction That Works*. Alexandria, VA: Association for Supervision and Curriculum Development.

Marzano, Robert, Pickering, Debra, and Pollock, Jane. (2001). *Classroom Instruction That Works*. Alexandria, VA: Association for Supervision and Curriculum Development.

McLaughlin, Maureen, and Allen, Mary Beth. (2002). *Guided Comprehension: A Teaching Model for Grades 3–8*. Newark, DE: International Reading Association.

Mills, Lauren. (1991). *The Rag Coat*. Boston: Little, Brown.

Mooney, Margaret. (2001). *Text Forms and Features*. Katonah, NY: Richard C. Owen.

Moustafa, Margaret. (1997). *Beyond Traditional Phonics*. Portsmouth, NH: Heinemann.

Murphy, Carlene, and Lick, Dale. (1998). *Whole-Faculty Study Groups: A Powerful Way to Change Schools and Enhance Learning*. Thousand Oaks, CA: Corwin.

Murray, Donald. (1990). *Shoptalk: Learning to Write With Writers*. Portsmouth, NH: Heinemann.

Nagy, William E. (1988). *Teaching Vocabulary to Improve Reading Comprehension*. Newark, DE: International Reading Association.

Napier, Matt, and Melanie Rose. (2002). *Z Is for Zamboni*. Chelsea, MI: Sleeping Bear Press.

National Academy of Education, Commission on Reading. (1984). *Becoming a Nation of Readers* (Prepared by R. C. Anderson, E. H. Hiebert, J. A. Scott, & I. A. G. Wilkinson). Washington, DC: National Academy of Education, National Institute of Education, and Center for Study of Reading.

Noe, Katherine Schick, Johnson, Nancy, and Hill, Bonnie Campbell. (1999). *Getting Started With Literature Circles*. Norwood, MA: Christopher Gordon.

O'Brien-Palmer, Michelle. (1999). *Graphic Organizers to Use With Any Book*. New York: Scholastic Press.

Optiz, Michael. (1998). *Flexible Grouping in Reading*. New York: Scholastic Press.

Optiz, Michael. (2000). *Rhymes & Reasons: Literature and Language Play for Phonological Awareness*. Portsmouth, NH: Heinemann.

Paulsen, Gary. (1987). *The Crossing*. New York: Laurel Leaf.

Pinnell, Gay Su, Fountas, Irene, and McCarrier, Andrea. (2000). *Interactive Writing: How Language and Literacy Come Together K–2*. Portsmouth, NH: Heinemann.

Polacco, Patricia. (1994). *Pink and Say*. New York: Philomel.

Portalupi, JoAnn, and Fletcher, Ralph. (1999). *Craft Lessons: Teaching Writing K–8*. Portland, ME: Stenhouse.

Portalupi, JoAnn, and Fletcher, Ralph. (2001). *Nonfiction Craft Lessons: Teaching Information Writing K–8*. Portland, ME: Stenhouse.

Portalupi, JoAnn, and Fletcher, Ralph. (2001). *Writing Workshop*. Portsmouth, NH: Heinemann.

Power, Brenda. (1999). *Parent Power: Energizing Home-School Communication*. Portsmouth, NH: Heinemann.

Rawls, Wilson. (1984). *Where the Red Fern Grows*. New York: Random House.

Readence, John, Moore, David, and Rickelman, Robert. (2000). *Prereading Activities for Content Area Reading and Learning*. Newark, DE: International Reading Association.

Rockwell, Anne F. (1977). *Albert B. Cub and Zebra: An Alphabet Storybook.* New York: Crowell.

Ruckman, Ivy. (1986). *Night of the Twister.* New York: Harper Trophy.

Schmoker, Mike. (2001). *The Results Fieldbook: Practical Strategies From Dramatically Improved Schools.* Alexandria, VA: Association for Supervision and Curriculum Development.

Scieszka, Jon. (1995). *The True Story of the Three Little Pigs by A. Wolf.* New York: Viking Kestrel.

Shephard, Lorrie A., and Smith, Mary Lee. (1989). *Flunking Grades: Research and Policies on Retention.* New York: Taylor & Francis.

Simon, Seymour. (1985). *Saturn.* New York: William Morrow.

Simon, Seymour. (2001). *Tornadoes.* New York: HarperCollins.

Sitton, Rebecca. (2002). *Spelling Sourcebook Series.* Scottsdale, AZ: Egger Publishing.

Smith, Wilma, and Andrews, Richard. (1989). *Instructional Leadership: How Principals Make a Difference.* Alexandria, VA: Association for Supervision and Curriculum Development.

Snow, Catherine, Burns, Susan, and Griffin, Peg. (Eds.). (1998). *Preventing Reading Difficulties in Young Children.* Washington, DC: National Academy Press.

Spandel, Vicki. (Ed.). (2001). *Books, Lessons, Ideas for Teaching the Six Traits: Writing in the Elementary and Middle Grades.* Wilmington, MA: Great Source Education Group.

Stead, Tony. (2002). *Is That a Fact? Teaching Nonfiction Writing K–3.* Portland, ME: Stenhouse.

Strickland, Dorothy, Ganske, Kathy, and Monroe, Joanne. (2002). *Supporting Struggling Readers and Writers: Strategies for Classroom Intervention 3–6.* Portland, ME: Stenhouse.

Strong, William. (1994). *Sentence Combining: A Composing Book.* New York: McGraw-Hill.

Strong, William. (1995). *Writer's Toolbox: A Sentence Combining Workshop.* New York: McGraw-Hill.

Strube, Penny. (1996). *Getting the Most From Literature Groups.* New York: Scholastic Press.

Taylor, Barbara. (2003). The CIERA Classroom Observation Scheme! Using Data on Reading Instruction to Improve Practice. Paper presented at the Colorado Council of International Reading Association.

Taylor, Barbara, Graves, Michael, and Van Den Broek, Paul. (2000). *Reading for Meaning: Fostering Comprehension in the Middle Grades.* Newark, DE: IRA & Teachers College Press.

Taylor, Barbara, Pearson, P. David, Clark, Kathleen, and Walpole, Sharon. (2000). Effective Schools and Accomplished Teachers: Lessons About Primary-Grade Reading Instruction in Low-Income Schools. *The Elementary School Journal,* 101(2), 121–165.

Terban, Marvin. (1983). *In a Pickle and Other Funny Idioms.* New York: Clarion.

Terban, Marvin. (1987). *Mad as a Wet Hen! And Other Funny Idioms.* New York: Clarion.

Terban, Marvin. (1990). *Punching the Clock: Funny Action Idioms.* New York: Clarion.

Terban, Marvin. (1998). *Scholastic Dictionary of Idioms.* New York: Scholastic.

Thompson, Gare. (2002). *A Whaling Community of the 1840s.* Washington, DC: National Geographic.

Tomlinson, Carol Ann. (1999). *The Differentiated Classroom: Responding to the Needs of All Learners*. Alexandria, VA: Association for Supervision and Curriculum Development.

Trelease, Jim. (2001). *Read Aloud Handbook*. 5th ed. New York: Penguin.

Turner, Ann. (1987). *Nettie's Trip South*. New York: Aladdin Library.

Von Hoff Johnson, Bonnie. (1999). *Wordworks: Exploring Language Play*. Golden, CO: Fulcrum Resources.

Waddell, Martin. (2002). *Owl Babies*. New York: Candlewick.

Wagstaff, Janiel. (1994). *Phonics That Work*. New York: Scholastic Press.

Wagstaff, Janiel. (1999). *Teaching Reading and Writing With Word Walls: Easy Lessons and Fresh Ideas for Creating Interactive Word Walls That Build Literacy Skills*. New York: Scholastic Press.

Weaver, Constance. (1996). *Teaching Grammar in Context*. Portsmouth, NH: Heinemann.

Wood, Margo, and Salvetti, Elizabeth Prata. (2001). Project Story Boost: Read-Alouds for Students at Risk. *The Reading Teacher*, 55(1), 76–83.

Wood-Walters, Darla. (1999). *Maximizing Your Students' Growth in Writing and Reading (Grades K–1)*. Bellevue: Bureau of Education & Research.

Zogby, Sharon. (1999). Seeds of Success: Workshops for Parents of Emergent Readers. *Illinois Reading Council Journal*, 27(1), 30–41.

Videos From the Bureau of Education & Research: (1–800–735–3503)

Increasing Students' SPELLING ACCURACY in Daily Writing Across the Curriculum: Part I: Keys to an Effective Spelling Program, Grades 1–6.

Increasing Students' SPELLING ACCURACY in Daily Writing Across the Curriculum: Part II: Effective Spelling Instruction, Grades 1–6.

State-of-the-Art Strategies for Teaching Writing.

Strengthening Students' Phonemic Awareness, Grades K–1.

Using GUIDED READING to Strengthen Students' Reading Skills at the Developing Level.

Using GUIDED READING to Strengthen Students' Reading Skills at the Emergent Level.

Using GUIDED READING to Strengthen Students' Reading Skills at the Fluent Level.

Using INTERACTIVE WRITING to Strengthen Your Students' Phonemic Awareness and Phonics Skills, K–1.

Using Literacy Centers to Strengthen Your Reading and Writing Program, Grades K–3.

Using Modeled Writing to Maximize Your Students' Growth in Writing and Reading, K–1.

Using ONSETS & RIMES AND MANIPULATION OF TEXT to Strengthen Your Students' Phonemic Awareness and Phonics Skills.

Using the MAKING WORDS Strategy to Strengthen Your Students' Phonemic Awareness and Phonics Skills.

Using Word Walls to Strengthen Students' Reading and Writing at the Early/Fluent Levels.

Using Word Walls to Strengthen Students' Reading and Writing at the Emergent Level.

Vocabulary Strategies That Boost Your Students' Reading Comprehension, Grades 2–6.

Index